OUTBACK OUTLAW

THE DARK LEGACY OF AUSTRALIA'S BACKPACKER KILLER, IVAN MILAT

RYAN GREEN

For Helen, Harvey, Frankie and Dougie

Disclaimer

This book is about real people committing real crimes. The story has been constructed by facts but some of the scenes, dialogue and characters have been fictionalised.

Polite Note to the Reader

This book is written in British English except where fidelity to other languages or accents are appropriate. Some words and phrases may differ from US English.

YOUR FREE BOOK IS WAITING

CONTENTS

Outlaw of the Outback

The world blurred sideways in the dark of the night. Neon and stars spun in a great kaleidoscope of colours. Liquor and beer churned in his stomach, and though deep inside of him he was still as sane and rational a man as he always had been, the only sound he could force out of his mouth was wild laughter.

Paul Onions was on his holidays.

The first few days had been the dullest, arriving in Sydney, scouting around for a place to sleep, then scouting again for a place to sleep that cost half as much so there'd be twice as much money for beer. The young air-conditioning engineer had managed to acquire a six-month travel visa to Australia, and he meant to see as much of that beautiful country as possible before his visa ran out.

For the past few weeks, he'd stayed in a backpacker's hostel in Kings Cross, Sydney. He liked that it cost only pennies to stay there. Liked that it was central enough that he could get right out the door and see the sights when he rolled out of bed. It sure beat camping out or sleeping rough, like he'd been worried he might have to on occasion. But the best part of a hostel, anywhere in the world, was the friends that you made while crammed into a space with new and different people. Given the limited space, everyone pretty much slept on top of one another and you couldn't help but see and hear each others comings and goings. It was like a boarding school dormitory for adults, so it was a small wonder that despite the language barriers, everyone ended up as friends. Or if not friends, at least close enough to go out for a drink with when nobody else was about.

By day they all went out sightseeing—visiting the local landmarks and wonders of the world—but by night when all the lazy Europeans finally rolled out of their beds and hangovers, the party started. Shots and beers. Cigarette smoke permeated every fibre of his clothes and every strand of his hair. Music pulsing and thumping to the rhythm of his heartbeat. There was nowhere in the world with a nightlife like Sydney's, and they were all only going to be there once in their lives. Was it any wonder that when the time came to party, they partied hard?

Partying was a little bit too hard for Paul's bank account, unfortunately.

He'd been saving up for a year to fund this backpacking trip, keeping every penny he made working part-time while he was a student, squirrelling away birthday money, Christmas gifts, everything he could scrape together. Before he'd even gotten on the plane, he had it all neatly divided into six chunks of spending money to get him through each month in Australia. Exactly what he needed to last until his flight back home. But that had been when the journey was abstract. When he'd thought that he'd be all alone, hiking and looking at big rocks and waving at kangaroos. Things that he still planned on doing, amazing things he'd never be able to do anywhere else in the world, but things that didn't cost any money. As it turned out, not travelling all over the place to see all the sights were a bit more expensive since partying doesn't come cheap. The trouble was, he was having one hell of a good time and he didn't want to let his new friends down or make them feel sorry for him and buy his drinks. He just wanted to have a good time. He was on the holiday of a lifetime—shouldn't he have a good time?

By night, he certainly thought so. When he was bouncing to the music and the pretty girls were smiling and the beer tasted good, he knew with absolute certainty enjoyed only by the young that this was what life was all about. But come morning, when his head pounded and his plans for the rest of his trip were coming apart at the seams, it occurred to him that he could have had half as good a time for twice as long and still been quite content. Even living frugally for the rest of his trip wasn't going to make ends meet. He'd eaten through months of savings in weeks. If he meant to keep on with his Australian adventure in any form, he needed a cash injection. His family back home were not going to send him money to drink. His friends had never been as smart with their money as him, probably because they weren't all planning a big blow-out trip to Australia.

If he wanted money, he was going to have to work for it. That had always been his philosophy in life, so he had no trouble getting up one morning, despite an agonizing hangover, to look for something he could turn his hand to that might help him pad out his dwindling savings.

At first, he went it alone, but a quick tour around town revealed that the one thing that Sydney was not lacking in was air-conditioner engineers. Everywhere had to be air-conditioned, and everyone had a guy they knew who handled it for them. Paul didn't know if it was one guy who worked like the devil, or if there was an engineer on every street corner. Regardless, there was no hope in hell of him getting a job in his field, and even less of a chance anyone was willing to pay him under the table considering he wasn't even certified to do the work by the local associations or unions.

So, he turned to his new friends for advice. Some of them had local friends who might be able to hook him up, others were hardcore backpackers who'd been travelling for years together, picking up odd jobs as they went to keep the train rolling long after what they'd put aside for their original trips had run dry.

The local friends couldn't do much to help him—it wasn't peak season for tourists, which meant that a lot of the part-time work that did pop up in Sydney just wasn't available. Even if it was, nobody was likely to hire a foreign worker when there were a ton of Australian kids ready and waiting who were far less liable to vanish overnight having decided they wanted to see a new town.

The full-time backpackers, though, had some solid ideas on what he could do to cover his costs. Most of them had picked up dozens of jobs over the years, filling in the gaps that every local economy had. All the jobs that locals didn't want to get their hands dirty with, or that didn't last long enough for the average person to be interested in committing to, were readily available to travellers if they just knew where to look, and his new friends, happily, knew just where to look.

The first thing to do was get out of the city. Cities had nothing for people like them. Cities were already packed to bursting with teenagers seeking weekend work, students slotting odd jobs and paid chores in around their schedules, not to mention the usual hordes of the unemployed that you could find anywhere. Suburbia was even worse—there were far fewer businesses, and the ones that were there were already overloaded with locals looking for an easy gig. No. If an itinerant worker wanted to find some money, and this was true pretty much anywhere in the world, they needed to head out into the country. There, the human population was much thinner and every individual who was willing to work suddenly came at a premium.

It was fruit picking season in the farms of New South Wales, and while there was usually an influx of labour from Asia to ensure nothing rotted on the vine, there was always room for more bodies in the fields. It paid poorly for how hard the work was, and when all the fruit was picked, the job was over and you had to move on. Nobody who lived locally wanted anything to do with that kind of work, but for Paul, it was perfect! He'd get away from the temptations of town, bank enough cash to cover him an extra month or two, and then jump right back into the party when his work was done. It seemed to be an ideal solution. Except he had no way to get out there to where the farms that needed workers were located. There was a bus service in town, but that only got you to suburbia. There were flights out of town, but that only took you to another city. If you wanted to get out into wild spaces between the cities, you needed somebody local to give you a ride. Walking was considered tantamount to suicide given the vast expanses of Australia that were devoid of human life. You could hike for an entire day and never see another living soul, never mind the scorching heat and potentially hostile indigenous wildlife.

The idea of taking a taxi was bandied around, but that only became economical if they could get a few people all heading out together, and even then, it would probably cost them a day's worth of wages or more. His friends weren't interested in looking for work since they still had plenty of money to play with, so it looked like Paul would be going it alone.

Still, despite these road bumps, Paul wasn't worried at all. The people of Australia were the nicest, friendliest, most welcoming folks he had ever met in his life, and he felt like he could trust them with just about anything. If he had to rely on the kindness of strangers to make his way to where he was going, then there wasn't a doubt in his mind he was going to make it there just fine. If the Australians he'd already met were any indication, they'd probably take him out for dinner and a few beers before dropping him off. These people were unreal, veritable living saints compared to the dour faces of home. He put it down to all the sunshine.

So, with all his plans laid out and his still-hungover friends sleeping it off in the hostel, Paul set out for the edge of town. He hopped buses until he made it to the furthest outskirts of suburbia, and then he casually strolled along the motorway. In the early morning, it felt just like home. The cool air tinged with a breath of the sea, the sun hanging low. He wasn't making any great progress along his way, but the plan wasn't to walk. Every time a car rolled by, he'd stick up his thumb and give them his most hopeful smile.

He didn't need all of them to stop, he didn't need most of them to stop, he just needed one.

But as the day stretched out, increasingly behind him, he began to question the wisdom of his plan. He knew the direction that he was headed was north, vaguely. He knew that he'd been heading that way all day. But looking out over the side of the road he could see nothing but forest and scrubland as far as the eye could see. The outback that he'd heard so much about didn't look so alien to his eyes. There were vast swathes of it that just looked like England—grass and trees, albeit a lot more of them. Here and there, there were some plants he didn't recognise or a birdcall he couldn't quite pinpoint but for the most part, the country was just the country. Nothing new. He was disappointed not to see a kangaroo or two roaming around, though if he'd thought about it, he probably would have realised the only kangaroos that hung around next to a busy road were roadkill.

The sun had passed its zenith and was creeping down towards the horizon, and still, he trudged on. He'd brought himself drinking water and some little snacks to tide him over until he arrived at his destination, but now for the first time, he was confronted with the cold reality that maybe nobody was going to pick him up at all.

It would be a long cold night out here. The weather might have been warmer than home in the daytime, but by night the autumnal season became ever more apparent. Paul had thought of Australia as nothing but sun-kissed beaches. He hadn't even brought a jacket along with him. He was starting to regret that now as his teeth began to chatter and, still, nobody stopped to pick him up.

This far out there was no sign that man had ever touched the land except the road he was still bumbling along. Just as he was about to give up hope, a silver four-by-four came rumbling to a halt at the side of the road, startling him out of his reverie. 'You need a ride?'

He smiled up at the man with his wide-brimmed hat and even wider grin. 'Oh thank you, thank you so much. I was worried I was going to be out here all night.'

'Ain't no need to worry about that. Folks around these parts take care of one another, even if you are some pom tourist stamping around and scaring up the snakes.'

Paul paled as he scrambled up into the truck's cab. 'Snakes?'

The man gave him a wide-eyed nod but broke down into laughter before he could pad the story any more. 'Man, you're easy. I'm just fooling with you. Ain't no snakes out there going to bother on the road. Not less they want to become flat snakes.'

'Well, thanks for the ride anyway. I didn't fancy standing out there until morning.'

'Ain't no problem, buddy...'

The moustachioed driver reached over to shake Paul's hand even as they picked up speed again, setting the car wobbling from side to side and making the hair on the back of Paul's neck stand up. Still, it was hardly polite to comment on someone's driving when they were offering you kindness. 'I'm Bill, what do they call you back in merry old England?'

'Oh, I'm Paul.' He winced as Bill crushed his hand in a leathery grip.

'Nice to meet you, Paul. I'm Bill,' the man repeated like he was reading his lines off a bad script. 'What brings you to my neck of the woods?'

'Well, I'm looking for work you see, out on the farms.' Paul found himself scrambling for a seatbelt as they tore along the motorway. 'I hear that they're looking for berry pickers for the harvest.'

Bill let out a deafening guffaw and slapped Paul on the chest, harder than was playful. 'Well damn mate, guess you aren't scared of a little hard work.'

Coughing, Paul managed to mumble out. 'As they say, no rest for the wicked.'

'Hah, no rest for the... I like that.' Another slap, one that Paul managed to lean away from enough to only catch in on the shoulder, where there was a bit more meat and a little less pain. Bill's broad grin slipped off his face in an instant, as though it had never been there at all. 'Course, you wouldn't catch me working out there with all those damned slant-eyes.'

It felt like he was waiting for Paul to say something. To argue back against the disgusting things that he was now saying. To his shame, Paul found that he couldn't. Just like he'd never been able to stand up to the bullies back at school, now he was confronted with this very real personification of all the vile opinions in the world, and he just stalled out. All he could think was that he didn't want to make the guy angry. He was doing him a favour, giving him a ride, it would be pretty rude to call him a disgusting bigot. It would have been hard. Awkward.

Bill kept on going after a pause to see if he'd be stopped, sinking further and further into his bitter rant. 'Migrants, they're ruining this country. Crawling out of their mud huts and coming over here where we've got civilisation so they can grab as much quick cash as they can before heading home. Looters, that's what I'd call them.'

Paul shifted uncomfortably in the seat. Bill was hoping he'd chime in, but he didn't think he could stomach faking his agreement. 'I don't know anything about that, I'm afraid.'

'Oh I ain't talking about you, mate, don't you worry. You poms, you've got hot and cold running water back home, roofs over your heads, cars. All the real civilisation stuff that sets us apart from the savages.' The smile was snapped back into place for a moment as he tried to reassure Paul, but it slipped again just a moment later. 'I don't mind you coming over and taking a job from a hard-working Aussie. Because your lot will pay it back when one of us comes over there. That's a fair trade. But the Blacks, and the Chinese and the Jews, they're parasites. They're ruining this country. That's what they're doing.'

'I'm just on holiday. I'm afraid I don't know anything about what's happening here.' That should have been enough to get them off the topic and move on to discussing anything else. It was as close as Paul had come to assert himself.

He wasn't sure how Bill was going to take it. There was a long lingering silence as he braced himself to be on the receiving end of the man's bellowing, but when Bill's words finally came, they were soft and quiet. Wheedling and ingratiating instead of confrontational. 'That's alright, mate. That's alright. Wouldn't expect you to. Wouldn't expect me to know what's going on where you're from either. The important thing is we white folks have got to look out for each other. That's why I picked you up. Sure as hell wouldn't have picked you up if I thought you were one of them Chinese.'

It wasn't working. No matter what Paul said, Bill kept on swinging it back around to how much he hated other races. Paul made one last desperate attempt at a new subject. 'Well, as I said, I do appreciate the ride. I don't suppose you know any farms out here that are hiring right now?'

'Course I do, course I do. I'll drop you out by one of them fruit farms north of the Belanglo where they're needing folk.' The smile was back, soothing despite knowing what lurked beneath the surface. It was fully dark now, and Paul probably wouldn't have been able to see it if it weren't for the sudden flare of a lighter as Bill lit a cigarette for himself. He offered one to Paul, who politely declined with a wave of his hand.

'Wonderful, thanks so much.'

Bill's face lit up with each puff of the cigarette, painting his face orange as a fresh ember. 'No worries, mate. No worries.'

Paul's worries did not go away miraculously after that statement. His backpack—he'd slung into the back of the car—was out of reach, and with it, anything he might have pulled out to fidget with. He was stuck there in the front with nothing to do except keep on talking, and he had absolutely nothing to say.

In all the time he'd been in Australia, not once had he felt foreign. There had been no culture shock, no language barrier. Now he was starting to realise that was because he had stayed put in the safe, sanitised parts of Australia. The parts were the same as back home in the same way that whole swathes of Spain and her surrounding islands felt like home because they were so full of British people mangling the local culture into something that felt more palatable. This might have been the first truly Australian person that he'd met. The first one to live out in places that weren't built entirely for the consumption of tourists, and he was surprised to learn just how frightening that was.

It wasn't that the man's accent was strange or that he looked at all different from anyone else—it was that Paul had no idea what was behind those flame-glazed eyes.

They sped relentlessly down the road through the night, Paul having no idea where they were or how far they had travelled. For that matter, he couldn't even hazard a guess at how far he had walked before getting a ride from this strange man beside him. It occurred to him that nobody knew where he was going or when he was coming back. Anything could happen to him right now, and it would be months before anyone even noticed he was missing.

This disconcerting thought seeped through him slowly, like he'd swallowed a hunk of ice and it was gradually melting in his gut little by little. He was in a truck in the middle of nowhere with a stranger who could say or do anything, and Paul would have no way to stop him.

'You know, we don't get many hitchhikers out this way anymore.'

Paul wet his lips before he attempted an answer to that. 'Why might that be?'

'Well, most local folks, they've got their cars. And most visitors, well they stick to their places. Y' know? The cities and the beaches. Not many tourists brave enough to come out here.'

The sides of the road were pressing in on them now. The trees loomed and stole away much of the night sky. These vast shadows whipped by too fast for him to understand them. His world narrowed down to the red glow of Bill's cigarette and the stretch of road captured in his headlights. Everything else was pitch black. Everything else was invisible. Barely knowable. Tremors were running through Paul that had nothing to do with the vibration of the car's engine and everything to do with this new world of terror he was sinking into. 'Well, I don't believe I've ever been accused of bravery before. I think I'm mostly just desperate.'

'Hah, you and me both, mate. Nobody's out here because they want to be. Ain't a place folks come to, it's a place folks go through, you know? Nothing here for them.' Bill's face was illuminated by the reddish glow from his cigarette with each drag he took. What was probably a normal placid expression became seemingly transformed into something bizarre and monstrous. 'Course, them that know the Belanglo can see the beauty of it. A place where you can do what you want with nobody about. Hunting's good if you know how to shoot. Hell, even if you can't shoot worth a damn, the hunting's still good.'

Paul turned his face away just so he didn't have to look at Bill anymore so that he could stare out into what little he could see of the forest and try to calm his nerves. Nature. Trees. Nice relaxing stuff. Nothing to be scared of out here. Nothing to worry about. He was just being anxious, and there wasn't any real need for it. Bill might be a little rough around the edges, but he was a nice guy, picking up hitchhikers and helping them out. Driving Paul out to a farm even though it was out of his way. He just needed to calm down. Get the conversation onto something safe and soothing. 'You know, it didn't even occur to me that people might hunt out here. I'd have thought it would be a nature preserve or something.'

'Nature preserve?' Bill's chuckle had a sinister edge to it that Paul did his very best to ignore. 'Only thing preserving you from nature out here is a gun. Kanga's will kick your guts out as soon as look you at them. Snakes will turn you inside out with a bite. Spiders will make you wish the snakes got you. You went wandering along the road up here as you did back by town, you'd never see morning again, mate.'

Paul suppressed another shiver and turned his gaze back to the road ahead, any hopes of escape into an imaginary arcadia gone as fast as they'd come. Now every tree branch he saw stretching out to the road was a striking snake. Every bush was a crouching kangaroo. 'I had no idea it was so dangerous.'

'Dangerous? Nah, mate, that's just natural for you.' Bill slapped him on the knee this time around, another solid enough blow to leave Paul aching. 'Ain't any more dangerous than gravity. You step off a cliff you're going to fall. You step into the bush, you're going to meet something that wants to snack on you. That's just the world. If you want to talk about danger, then you need to start talking about the folks that live out there. Crazies, the lot of them.'

The cigarette that had been painting Bill's face with light died down. Consumed. He became a dull silhouette in the moonlight. Paul couldn't tell if he was grinning again. Couldn't tell how much of the man's words could be believed. 'Are you pulling my leg again?'

There was nothing jovial in his driver's tone when he answered. 'Wish I was, mate.'

The fear he'd been trying to ignore throughout the whole ride was back now, and it was back with a vengeance. The hair on his arms was standing up as he stared out into the night. He feared that should he turn around and look at Bill, he might see something he didn't like. Like he was in some creepy ghost story where instead of a phantom hitchhiker, the phantom was the one in the driver's seat. He fumbled on with the conversation—anything was better than sitting in deathly silence. 'So, real people are living out there in that jungle?'

'More than you'd think, mate. Folks living off the land, keeping to themselves, ducking the law.' Bill revved the engine, already in top gear but pumping so much fuel that Paul was amazed he hadn't flooded her. 'Outback, yeah? That's where the outlaws hide out.'

That ghost-story feeling came back. Because that was what this whole thing reminded Paul of. Sitting around a campfire, telling each other scary stories in the dark. That's what Bill was doing, spinning yarns to spook him. That was all it was. And he was falling for it, like the sap he was. 'Folks out there will rob you soon as you look at them. Ought to be careful with yourself.

Don't go wandering too far from town. Don't go taking rides from strangers.'

Paul refused to give in to his fear. He didn't let the other man intimidate him again with his scary stories about murderous kangaroos and venomous everything else. Rural murderers. Criminals in the outback. It was all just a fanciful yarn intended to wind him up again and he wasn't falling for it.

He forced a smile onto his face. 'You know, taking all that into account, given all the awful people I might have met out here at night, I'm very lucky to have found you.'

'Oh no, mate,' He slapped his hand down on Paul's leg again. Just long enough for it to become uncomfortable. 'I'm the one who was lucky to find you.'

Bill's words hung in the air. Not echoing, but lingering. Stretching out for what felt like hours. 'What do you mean, Bill?'

'My name's not Bill.'

Paul's mind was already consumed by anxiety at this point. They could be anywhere on the map and he would be none the wiser. They could have been on the moon and, looking through the windshield, he wouldn't be able to tell. He was in an unfamiliar place with a stranger who'd just admitted that everything Paul thought he knew about him was a lie. What came next? More lies? Or something much worse, the final revelation that they'd both been trying to avoid—Paul, because it meant all his fears would be fulfilled, and 'Bill' because it meant that he could no longer toy with the British boy as if he were some unfortunate little trapped mouse.

It was almost a relief to see the glint of gunmetal on the driver's lap. At least it meant that all the confusion was over... 'Don't know that you've ever been robbed before, but it's real simple. I figure you'll take to it like a natural, mate.'

A robbery, that was all this was. A robbery. He didn't need to be scared. He just needed to do what he was told when he was told, and he'd come out of this alright. Maybe not unscathed. Maybe not with everything he started with. But alive. And alive was all that mattered.

The truck, which had until now been roaring along the road at full speed and showing no signs of slowing, rolled to a halt, bumping off the tarmac and onto a dirt mound by the roadside. The Belanglo State Forest loomed, blocking the moon and stars from sight, leaving Paul all alone in the world with his saviour-turned-captor. 'What... what do you want me to do?'

'I'll be keeping your bag in case you've got anything good hidden in there, but you need to get every penny you've got out of your pockets right now. Lose that watch of yours, too.'

Paul started fumbling for his wallet. His jeans were too tight—when he tried to pull them out, they stuck into his side. Too panicked, he kept on pulling even though it couldn't go anywhere. 'Whatever you say.'

Bill reached over and grabbed him by the ear, peering at it for a moment, as though there might be treasure buried inside, before shoving him off. 'You poms are all like women. You got any jewellery on?'

Paul yelped as his chest hair was ripped out by Bill's grasping hands, tearing his shirt down the front to look for a necklace. 'No, I don't wear any...'

The gun dug into the side of his temple, cold metal in the humid night air. Paul's breath caught in his throat. He froze in place. 'Hurry up. Wallet. Money. Don't try and hide anything or I'll have to go looking for it. And you don't want that, do you, mate?'

He arched his back to grab for his wallet, only to jam against the seatbelt he'd so diligently fastened. He undid it as quickly as he could. 'Sorry. Right. Yes.'

The gun jabbed into his shoulder. 'Hurry it up.'

'I'm trying to...' His breath was coming again, fast and frantic, as his heart fluttered like a rabbit's. The cabin of the pickup seemed to spin around him as terror set in. It all seemed so unreal. How could this be happening to him? How could this be happening at all? As his eyes rolled, they abruptly stopped on one detail that froze him entirely.

The gun—it made sense. If you were going to rob someone, you needed a way to threaten them. In a weird way, that made the gun less terrifying. It was merely a prop, part of the set dressing of a mugging. But the rope that Paul had spotted coiled up on the back seat—that was something else – that didn't speak to a mere robbery. The only reason you'd need that was if you were tying someone up. The only reason you'd tie someone up is as if you were keeping them. If he was going to be kept, that meant this wasn't a mugging. He didn't know what it was, but oh god, it wasn't just a simple mugging.

Bill, or whatever his real name was, cocked the hammer on his revolver and levelled it at Paul's face. 'I said hurry your ass up, mate. Or I'm going to...'

To Paul's knowledge, he never made a conscious decision to run. He didn't remember reaching for the door handle. He didn't remember flinging himself out of the truck into the dirt as the first bullet careened by, overhead. He was starting to come back to himself as he rounded the back of the truck. Starting to think again. The blackness of terror that had completely consumed his mind, was now receding enough for him to gain at least some awareness of what was happening around him.

He ran. Both because his legs were already in fully-fledged motion and because even as he settled back into control of his body, he regretted it. As his awareness was re-established, he gratefully acknowledged that instinct had already fully committed his legs to that motion. Less welcome was the realization that with his burgeoning awareness, he would need to think of how to escape his current predicament. In a way, he resented that. What was the point of having instincts if they couldn't be relied on to carry him out of a situation like this? He didn't want to have to think. The thinking was a slow, ponderous process. Especially when compared to the speed of a bullet. He rushed along the road, ducking each time he heard another shot fired from behind him. Dropping to all fours, then scrambling back to his feet when he realised that he was still alive and hadn't been hit.

A car was headed along the motorway, and he frantically waved to it. Another shot pealed out, and he dived into the dirt once more. He was bleeding and scraped now, pain nipping at his arms and knees, but it wasn't important. The only thing that mattered was getting out of there alive.

In the distance, over the sound of the cars speeding by and completely ignoring him, Paul heard a sound that made his blood run cold. Bill was laughing. There was a cruelty to it, a mocking, but beneath that was the far more frightening amusement. The laugh wasn't frightening because of the harsh bark of it, or the way it made light of this life-and-death situation—it was frightening because it sounded like Bill was having a genuinely good time. This was his idea of a fun evening. That taking potshots at a guy after robbing him was every bit as humorous to him as good as a joke. That Paul's life was nothing but a punchline.

He wasn't going to die like that.

When the next car came tearing along the road, Paul threw himself out in front of it. If he was going to die one way or another and if his choice was suicide or joke, he'd take the front grill of that people carrier anytime. The woman driving it slammed on her brakes, skidding along the road. She would have hit him if he hadn't staggered backwards, unstable on his feet.

In an instant he was by the side of the car, pushing his way in beside her, shoving her oldest kid along and bellowing at the top of his lungs. 'Drive! Drive!'

She tried to push him out—the kids were all screaming, this was insane. But slowly as they wrestled, she took in the sight of him, the blood, the terror. She started to hear what he was yelling, loud enough to be heard over the voices of her children. 'He's trying to kill me! Please get me out of here! He's got a gun! You've got to help me.'

When she met his gaze, she saw real terror there. She heard his words, and through all the chaos, the meaning of those words cut through. She turned back to the windshield, to the parked truck at the roadside. To the man standing there, something metal glinting in the moonlight. He was raising it. He was pointing it at her. At her car. At her family.

Paul's instincts might have let him down in the middle of his flight, but hers seemed to be more finely tuned. She stamped down onto the accelerator and slammed her arm into the stranger's chest to stop him from being flung from his seat. Then they were off. Zero to a hundred as quick as lightning thanks to the reflexes of a mother whose children were in mortal danger. There was a bang from behind them that might have been a gun or might have been a car backfiring, either way, they would certainly never be going back to check.

The children were screaming as Paul was blubbering his thanks. The driver seemed to be completely deaf and dumb as she stared unflinchingly at the road ahead. She kept a white-knuckled grip on the wheel as she swerved through a U-Turn and headed back for the lights and safety of the city.

Everything was chaos, but it was the chaos of a car full of living breathing people, and if anything had played out even a little differently, then it might not have been.

The Family Milat

Two days after Christmas, 1944, Stjepan and Margaret Milat received a late gift. They already had four children by the time this little bundle of joy arrived, and Ivan would be the fifth of what soon grew to be a family of fourteen children.

Stjepan, known as Stephen to his Australian co-workers, was a Croatian immigrant who, since his arrival, had made his living in New South Wales, Australia, as a labourer on various work sites. His piecemeal career was mostly in the building trade, but, given an opportunity, he would turn his hand to almost any endeavour. Hard work was central to his ethos and having worked hard throughout his lifetime, he had built the physical strength to achieve almost any task he undertook...

Despite his diligence when it came to working, and his drive to constantly seek out new opportunities for himself, or perhaps because of that drive, he found his personal life to be somewhat lacking. He would drink and chat with those that he shared work with, but he had no real long-lasting friendships in Australia.

His itinerant working life effectively prevented him from settling into any place for long enough to put down roots.

He came from a large family, back in Croatia, and had always relied upon familial connections for his social life. There was always some cousin, brother-in-law or sister hosting family meals, and celebrations of births, marriages, and funerals were a near-weekly occurrence thanks to the volume of inter-connected families. Severed from that support network, he had become somewhat solitary.

His journey from that familiar place had come in the wake of the Great War, in which Stjepan had served with the British Army. As a result of that service, he found that he was now welcome as a resident anywhere in the Commonwealth, a marked difference from the usual immigration policies that were applied to his people. Seizing on the opportunity that was offered to him, he headed south as far as he could go. All the way south, to the very bottom of Australia.

Accordingly, it should come as no surprise that he was still single and alone at the age of thirty-four, given that his entire experience of relationships and marriage was built on that very old-world framework where friends of the family of similar ages were flung together with the expectation that they should pair off and produce the next generation. Not quite arranged marriage, but not quite the chaos of the dating scene either.

He had very traditional values, built up around his Catholic faith, endeavouring to attend church every Sunday even when it created problems in his work life such as being unavailable for those valuable time-and-a-half Sunday shifts. His commitment to his faith, however, eventually paid off in a big way when one fine Sunday, he met a girl by the name of Margaret Elizabeth Piddleston.

She was perfect, at least in his eyes. Young and beautiful, from a middle-class family with innumerable branches on its family tree, providing some semblance of the happy life that he had once known. What was more, she seemed to be quite taken with him as well. While his advances might have been seen as crude or clumsy by the more sophisticated women in his age bracket, this sixteen-year-old girl found them to be wildly romantic.

While there may have been some initial concern about the age gap among her family, Stjepan soon began to win them over with his obvious dedication to her, and the immense respect that he showed to his elders. The fact that he seemed to be a complete gentleman with no interest in pursuing anything but a traditional marriage, in which she would be well taken care of and have nothing to worry about but the raising of children, served well to ingratiate him to her conservative parents. He soon found himself recounting his old stories from Croatia with a certain nostalgia for better times in the history of the world, when communities pulled together and cared for each other. When men were men, doing a hard day's graft in exchange for their pay and making no complaints. He appealed to the ideal of the perfect husband in their minds, and so when he asked them for permission to propose to Margaret, they were happy to consent.

The couple were wed the same year, and by the end of that first year of marriage, Margaret's teenage body had already begun to distend with the first of their many babies, giving birth shortly before her seventeenth birthday to the first of their daughters. She would go on to have child after child with Stjepan, year after year, swelling and wilting over and over. He missed having his brothers and sisters around him and had no intention of letting his children suffer through the same isolation. Not to mention that his faith prevented the use of contraceptives regardless of how he felt about family planning.

When they were first married, the two of them settled into a house in the suburb of Guildford, twenty kilometres out from the centre of Sydney. But as their family continued to grow, they had to relocate time and time again. First to Bossley Park, even further out from civilisation, and then Liverpool, right on the very periphery of the city's expansion, within walking distance of the outback and all the freedom and danger that place represented. For Stjepan, it was ideal. He had grown up hunting for food in rural Croatia, and this represented a perfect return to form for him. He had purchased many guns over the years, and now that he had sons, he began teaching them how to shoot as soon as they were old enough to walk unaided.

All of the family contributed, whether they liked it or not. All the boys would set out hunting in the morning at sunrise and all the girls put to work around the house. It seems that misogyny was not one of the family's defining characteristics, however, as those tasks could be exchanged if it pleased both parties. In those early years, before Stjepan found more and more work for the children to be saddled with, they only had to help out until they'd contributed enough to satisfy their mother's far more lenient demands on them. The boys would often have enough game caught by mid-morning to provide more than enough food for the whole family. The girls would often have only a little light housework to catch up on that they could knock out in an hour or two, though the older ones tended to hold back and help in the kitchen a little later, just for the fun of cooking with their mother.

The children did attend school once they were of age, but none of them seemed to have any particular interest in it. They found the environment entirely too stifling compared to the freedom that their outdoorsy life usually afforded them. It wasn't so much that they were disruptive as they were disengaged. They'd learn things, but almost incidentally rather than as a direct result of teaching. They weren't the brightest of kids for the most part, predominantly because they couldn't bring themselves to focus on their studies. The only exception to this rule was Ivan himself. He had no more interest in school than any of the others, but he seemed to have a natural acuity that let him work his way through to his solutions when presented with a problem by his teachers. Furthermore, he seemed to passively absorb what was being said around him a lot more efficiently than any of his brothers and sisters. He'd still spend most of the school day messing around or staring out the window, but when he was called on to answer a question about the material, he still managed to produce the right answer. It was a source of constant irritation for his teachers that he was so obviously capable of excelling but unwilling to put in the work to do so.

Truancy was an ongoing problem among the Milat children, as they'd often go wandering in the outback, hunting or playing, rather than heading in the opposite direction and going to school. Even once they were in school there was nothing short of locking them inside the classroom that could guarantee that they'd remain there, and when one of them went walkabout, the others would almost invariably follow. They had few friends outside of their family group, and they seemed to want it that way. The siblings all watched out for one another, standing up for each other against the other students or any figure of authority, even when it actively made things worse for them.

Through their upbringing and the close-knit structure of their family, they became isolated from everyone around them. Not deliberately ostracised, but not invited around for dinner either. Their behaviour was simply too unpredictable. One day a Milat child might chat away happily with a classmate only to beat them to the ground the next day. They operated as a law unto themselves, and it became clear early on that appealing to the parents for help was not liable to produce the results that they might like. Margaret insisted that her children had just fallen in with a rough crowd, and that was what was prompting their ill behaviour, even though the only crowd that they moved in was their own. The father, meanwhile, responded to every complaint about his children by sending them in the next day bruised and battered. It was not a solution that anyone wanted.

Catholic or not, there was only one higher power in the Milat household, and its name was Stjepan. He did not care for any authority but his own, and he inflicted that authority on his children whenever he felt like it was being flouted. Should any one of the children come home from school with a bad report, they would be struck down with the back of his hand. Should any of them come back in from playing and a neighbour make a complaint about their behaviour, once again, the back of his hand would drive the child to the floor. Given that, more often than not, the kids all played together and got into mischief together, this meant that they all suffered the same plight, lining up to take the blow and only earning some glimmer of begrudging respect from their father if they took a hit without falling.

Ivan was the one who could best take a hit before falling. He was the one who'd scowl right back at his father while he was taking his berating and his beating. It didn't seem to occur to either party that this approach wasn't working. Ivan and his siblings seemed to consider the blows they suffered to be the price of having a good time. Stjepan never seemed to realise that no matter how many times he bludgeoned his children to the floor, they'd just get right back up again and go back to doing whatever the hell they wanted.

With all discipline left to him, Margaret got to serve a different role. He was the harsh realities of the world outside, and she was the kindness of home and family. No matter what report she heard from friends, neighbours, or her husband himself, she simply could not believe anything bad about her children. In her eyes, they were perfect and pure and incapable of doing anything wrong. It went beyond her refusal to believe bad reports from the schools and extended out into complete and wilful denial of reality.

The truth was that the Milat children were a closed group of kids abiding only by their own rules of behaviour. Running riot through the wilds and suburbia alike. The police got to know them from a very young age, but the sheer volume of sons and daughters often made it near impossible to identify which particular Milat was in trouble at any given time unless they laid hands on them. And that was something that only rarely occurred since nobody knew their way around like those kids.

They knew shortcuts to places most folks didn't even know existed. They could be on one street one minute and deep in the bush the next. Adding to the confusion was the fact that they all looked so much alike that spotting kids in entirely different places might simply have meant that entirely different kids were in those different locations rather than one clever child evading capture by using a cunning shortcut. To anyone chasing them, it was like trying to find a needle in a haystack, if the haystack were also made of needles and every needle in the needle stack was actively sprinting in a different direction while gesturing at you rudely.

For the most part, it was the ten boys who got into trouble the most frequently. All the children covered for each other, to the extreme of telling blatant lies to the police, family, and neighbours, but the girls seemed to receive special protection even on top of that. It was almost sweet, how deeply the brothers seemed to care for their sisters, though it was also possible that they had correctly intuited that they'd be blamed for any misbehaviour their sisters were caught in and suffer even more severe consequences as a result.

After a period of bouncing between jobs even more than usual, Stjepan found a new permanent position for himself as a wharf labourer in Liverpool, handling the material that skipped the big harbour of Sydney and came up the Georges River from the coast—something that unfortunately precipitated another move for the whole family.

In some ways, the new home was better than the last, at least in the eyes of Stjepan. It was even more isolated and rural than their previous home, even smaller, too, so that all fourteen of the children were stacked in triple bunk beds spread across only two bedrooms. But the primary appeal was all of the arable lands that came with the property. At last, Stjepan could start farming again, as he had in his youth. All the money that they were wasting on food could, at last, be channelled to other expenses... What was more, all the freeloading children would finally start contributing to the household.

The children knew better than to object when their daily chores went from light work around the house to working a full crop farm. Margaret was dragged into the work as well but mostly served in a supervisory role. After years of rough and wild living, the boys had more than enough strength to match anything that an adult might be expected to cope with. Any tasks that they could not cope with individually, they could handle as a group. Any that they couldn't handle as a group, they struggled and strained to get through, accepting the pain as necessary. Suffering was a part of their lives that they had simply come to accept.

Now that they were almost all at school, they also learned to accept that a lack of sleep was sometimes necessary. Their workload did not differ from school time and the holidays. Crops still needed to be harvested and planted regardless of how they spent their days. Whatever social life they might have entertained before was now stripped away as they left behind all childish things and instead gave themselves over to working the fields. The average bedtime for the Milat kids became 2 am during school time. They would be out in the dead of night watering tomatoes and planting seed potatoes.

Interspersed with this, they were still expected to keep up their hunting and housework. They went from trading chores as they used to, to a system of specialisation, with the strongest taking on the heavier tasks, the best shooters heading out into the bush to catch the game, and the rest dividing the labour based on whoever could get it done the most efficiently.

Ivan found himself switching between roles regularly. He was a sharpshooter from an early age, so there was an obvious benefit to having him hunting. He was strong for his age so that, even though he was the fourth oldest, he could hold his own in feats of strength against his older siblings. More importantly, he had a head for numbers that made him invaluable in planning out the work. No matter what he turned his hand to around the farm, that was the area that most excelled that day.

He established himself as a leader among the children as well as being the child most respected by the parents. It would have been nice if this role had been granted to him exclusively due to his excellence, but it seems that was not the case. He may have been stronger, smarter, and better equipped to deal with the challenges of their everyday life, but the way that he ensured his dominance was the same way that his father had demonstrated his dominance, day after day, throughout their entire lives - through unrestrained violence.

The boys would fight, as all boys are prone to, but where the others would be satisfied after someone walked away with a black eye, Ivan was devoted to brutality. He would break bones. He would beat his siblings until they could no longer stand under their own power. It was the only way that he knew how to keep them obedient, so it was what he did. While you might think that this would lead to resentment and hatred from his siblings, they viewed it as an expression of the natural order of things, with the strong lording over the weak. They had been raised in a sort of social Darwinism by their father, so it was hardly surprising that they adopted it as a core belief.

In much the same way that wolves select an 'alpha' based on who is the most vicious and willing to harm others in the group, so too was Ivan elected to be the leader of this pack.

The market farming endeavour that Stjepan had forced them all to undertake did not prove to be fruitful. He was never able to get a decent rate for any of the crops that his family produced, and they remained entirely reliant upon his wages to make ends meet. Whatever dream he may have had of subsisting off the land, or even thriving off the grid, soon fell away into the drudgery of the work itself. Now that they had invested so much into the crops, there was no way that they could stop farming without taking a loss, and they were not affluent enough to absorb that sort of loss. So even though it was getting them nowhere and leaving all of them exhausted, the endless grind of work had to continue.

The net result of this constant financial drag was that as soon as it was legal to do so, Ivan's older siblings dropped out of school and took on work. It would still be quite some time before he was allowed to do so, but Ivan seemed to baulk at the restrictions placed on him even more than before now that he felt like the end was in sight. Truancy among the Milat children was at an all-time high by the time he was heading into his teenage years, as they all followed his lead in this as in everything else. Yet it was his extra-curricular activities that would shape his education from that point forward.

As much as any one of the Milat kids was willing to take a slap on the wrist for any of the others when serious consequences were being handed down to them, Ivan seemed to be the only one with the courage to face them. When a whole posse of Milat boys were arrested for theft, he was the one to step up and claim responsibility. He was the mastermind, he had been the one to do the actual crime, and the others were just lookouts for him, bullied into it by their older brother. Innocent of all crimes. The police didn't believe for a second that Ivan alone was responsible, but at this point, having any of them up on charges felt like a miracle, and Ivan shouldering the blame and making a confession to that effect allowed them to finally dole out some long-delayed punishment.

Misspent Youth

At the age of thirteen, three years before he could drop out of school entirely, he was placed into the care of the Boy's Town residential school for the children of those unable to handle their unruly or neglected children. It was, essentially, a prison for those too young to be placed into a real prison, but because it was not a 'real' prison, sentencing was not for a set term. Until graduation, he would remain confined on the school grounds, sleeping in the school dormitories, attending classes, and working the fields around the institution. It was the kind of hard labour that would break the spirit of most budding young criminals, convincing them that life on the straight and narrow was the only way that they could escape such torment in the future. For Ivan, it was a long overdue holiday. Without distraction, he excelled in all his classes, slept well, and ate three hot meals a day. Even the farm labour he was assigned was markedly less than he was accustomed to back home. He didn't even feel like he was missing out socially as he soon developed the same position for himself among the other inmates as he had among his siblings. The ones he wasn't smarter than, he was stronger than. The ones he wasn't stronger than, he was smarter than. And the one who were both stronger and smarter just couldn't hold a candle to his willingness to harm others to get his way. Once more, he ascended the hierarchy and made himself a king amongst children. The biggest fish in a very small pond.

For almost two years, he remained a captive of the state in New South Wales, enduring the worst punishment that could be bestowed upon him by law as though it were nothing more than a joke. Compared to his home life, it was. Even when guards overstepped and inflicted corporal punishment, it was like a slap on the wrist compared to the beatings he would have had to endure back home. The only thing that he missed was the company of his sisters, which he could not so easily replicate in this environment. In particular, he missed the company of his youngest sister, Margaret Junior, to whom he had developed a particular attachment. He would have done anything to help out his brothers, anything to help out his sisters—that was part and parcel of being their leader— but that did not mean that he felt he owed them any kindness. He did what was expected of him and no more. The only one who ever really saw a softer side to him was little Margaret, whom he doted on, taking on her chores as his own, stealing little gifts for her and generally cherishing her as much as it was possible for anyone his age to care for a younger sibling. They would write, intermittently, throughout his imprisonment, but neither one of them had any particular talent with the written word, so these communications tended towards the dry and shallow. Neither one expressed how they truly felt, at least on paper.

At this point it probably bears mentioning that there were, and still are, rumours circulating that the Milat children were engaged in incestuous relationships with one another. Some criminologists have offered up the supposition, that as the 'alpha' among the male children, Ivan was accustomed to having his pick of the girls. While it has not been possible to substantiate these rumours with anyone present to bear witness, for obvious reasons, this theory has been included in this book simply to elaborate on the potential relationships between the various children during that time. It is certainly plausible, given their isolation from society at large, the us-versus-them mentality that was prevalent among the Milats, and particularly in light of the children's lack of access to any typical dating pool as a result of their criminality and reputations, that they may have engaged in such unconventional relationships.

While the lack of any evidence beyond the mumbling of the usual rumour mill suggests that, perhaps, no incest took place, the prevalence of such rumours still serves to illustrate that the relationships between the various siblings were so unnaturally close that the rumours might not have come as any big surprise had such relationships been irrefutably confirmed. No physical affairs may have been going on, but the children were emotionally closer to one another than most people are to their lovers and spouses as adults.

Their mother was oblivious to them. Their father was a harsh taskmaster. The rest of the world had decided from the very beginning that they'd never amount to anything more than back-country trash. But so long as they had one another, the Milat children still considered their lives to be good.

After his release from Boy's Town, Ivan returned to the family home, to his distant, cold father, his overbearing mother and the siblings that alternated between worshipping him and fearing him. After his time institutionalised, he had adopted many of his father's old mannerisms without even realising it. The enforced order of his imprisonment had left him with the same obsessive need for cleanliness and desire for order that afflicted his father and made him so demanding. He couldn't do much to tame the chaos of the communal bedrooms, but he took to household chores with a new ferocity that seemed to delight his mother as well as his younger siblings, to whom most of that work still fell.

All of the older siblings dropped out of school as soon as it was legal and sought out work for themselves—the boys primarily as day labourers, the girls taking any role they could find. Ivan himself began picking up work on the building sites, filling in any empty time between jobs with other work on the local farms where he could. The family was always struggling for money, and he had no hesitation in taking on any task if it might bring some more in. If he could have taken a job by his father's side, then he would have, gladly, but the work was not to be had, especially for a teenager. None of the grown men at the docks would have stood for nepotism when they all had family looking for good work, and none of them would have believed that a boy of barely sixteen would have the strength to stand beside them and bear the burdens they bore. He could have. Even before the years of hard labour, Ivan could have matched them crate for crate by the force of his determination alone.

There still wasn't enough money. Ends never met. They always struggled while Stjepan ignored them all and Margaret tried to ignore what was happening, head planted firmly in the sand. It was hardly surprising that the children who had grown up being told that they were nothing but criminals and would amount to nothing more did turn to crime.

It had started small enough, burglaries and robberies that barely made the papers. Scraping in with a few lines just before the sports section. The local police blamed it on the Milat children every time, just as they always had, but this was not the kind of petty trouble they'd been involved with as kids, it was the kind of serious crime that would put them away in jail, and that required serious evidence to back it up, not just suspicion and hearsay.

Ivan had learned a lot from his time in Boys Town. Not just the necessity of cleanliness and order in his life, but how to commit real crimes, and how to steal without being caught. Ultimately, like so many of these institutions, Boy's Town had turned into a trade school for criminals, and Ivan had learned his lessons well.

With each crime, his confidence grew. With every success, he grew bolder in plotting the next—because although every one of the Milat children was involved in these robberies to some degree, he was their leader. The one who laid the plans and smoothed out the wrinkles when mistakes were made.

As it turned out, he was also the one who would still shoulder the consequences when things went completely wrong.

Throughout the 1960s, Ivan was in and out of jail, spending probably as much time incarcerated as he did out on the streets. His brothers would sometimes end up in there with him, but more often than not, he would provide the police with a sufficient confession to keep anyone else from becoming involved. Their favoured crime by that point was stealing cars that they'd then sell along to friends in the scrapyards for their parts. It was good money, and the legitimate businesses buying the cars absorbed much of the burden of risk in reselling their ill-gotten gains—an arrangement that worked out fine for all of them but still never quite seemed to bring in enough money to make all the danger and effort truly worthwhile.

Ivan served several sentences in prison as their crimes escalated, each longer than the last but prison had no effect on him. He was not able to dominate others in his surroundings so easily in adult prisons, where peers grouped, but neither was he anyone's target. If anything, these periods seemed to serve as a holiday from his usual life rather than a deterrent.

He went on happily shouldering the burdens of guilt until he and his brothers graduated to armed bank robbery.

Armed robbery in itself was not something far outside of their usual remit— every child in the Milat house had been born to the gun and raised to have one with them at all times. Personal experience had taught them that the world was a violent and unforgiving place and that survival was the only thing that mattered. The vast majority of the burglaries that they had carried out had been committed while carrying weapons, just in case. The muggings had involved threats of violence, and even their car thefts were undertaken with an arsenal in tow.

What was unusual was the fact that they were targeting a high-risk institution like a bank. Someplace with security would require a lot of planning to successfully circumvent. Not to mention the increased publicity and danger involved for everyone who participated.

The robbery did not go smoothly. Though they successfully intimidated the customers, the tellers were not as obedient as they desired, and the vault was inaccessible without the manager, who then managed to secrete himself away and call for assistance. The Milat boys were confronted by armed police as they emerged from the front of the bank, and just like they had when they were kids caught in the act, they scattered, every one of them sprinting off in a different direction. One going for the alleyway, one going for their get-away car, another sprinting off down the street. It hadn't been planned, but it worked. The police had to divide their attention, chasing multiple targets instead of one, and they were unwilling to fire on suspects unless they were being attacked first. They bellowed threats after the Milats, but after a lifetime of receiving empty threats of violence, none of them seemed to quite believe them. Of the bank robbers, only a single one was caught. And this time, it wasn't Ivan.

His younger brother shouldered the full weight of responsibility for the robbery, refusing to say a single word about his co-conspirators. His refusal to cooperate with the judicial system in bringing others to justice meant that he, alone, would shoulder the full wrath of that system. Even though the burden of finding evidence that his brothers were involved in the robbery lay with the police, the judicial system resented the boy's refusal to turn on his kin. The maximum sentence possible for a first offence was handed down and he was summarily sent off to prison.

This was not the only person who ended up in jail over crimes committed that day, nor the only one to suffer consequences. While his brothers took off running in random directions, Ivan remained cool and calm, strolling a street away and climbing into the back of a taxi driven by Neville Knight. He growled out a random destination to the driver so as not to lead any investigation back to his home, then he sat quietly in the back as Knight did his job. If Knight had known that there was a bank robber or a weapon in the back of his car, he gave no account of it later. He did not even remember Ivan's face. All that he knew was he had picked up a fare, driven the man to where he wanted to go, and then, without warning, his world had exploded into pain.

Seated behind the taxi driver, Ivan had stealthily drawn out his sawn-off shotgun and positioned it against the back of the driver's seat. When the time came to pay his fare, he elected instead to pull the trigger thereby eliminating a potential witness.

The shrapnel of the car seat, combined with the shotgun pellets, tore through Knight's spine and he slumped forward over the wheel, appearing entirely dead. Ivan then left the vehicle without a second glance, and it would be several minutes before a bystander came to investigate the still-running taxi with a driver slumped over.

Knight survived, though he was entirely paralyzed from the neck down, despite enduring arduous bouts of surgery intended to repair the damage that had been done. Thanks to the horrific trauma he'd just suffered, he could remember absolutely nothing about the events that had preceded his injury, and the police failed to connect his shooting with the events at the bank earlier in the day. Instead, they proceeded to arrest a man named Allan Dillon who, despite being innocent of committing this heartless act of brutality, was promptly convicted and served five long years in prison. Compounding this injustice, the fact that he steadfastly refused to admit culpability for this violent crime rendered him unable to apply for parole.

If Ivan felt any guilt over the imprisonment of his younger brother or over the fate of the cab driver and the man convicted of shooting the cab driver, he did his best not to show it.

Showing any weakness in front of his family was considered to be extremely foolish, and guilt over the fate of his brother would have told his family that Ivan was a soft touch when it came to his siblings. It would have robbed him of his authority if they knew just how much he cared about them.

The next bank robbery went off without a hitch, every detail of Ivan's plan carried out to precision. No mistakes, no hidden managers, no police. Yet for all that, the police still suspected Ivan and his family were responsible. The expertly executed plan had been nearly identical to the one that they'd originally carried out, the meticulous planning a hallmark of Ivan's involvement. The noose began to tighten around Ivan even though no actual evidence could be found to implicate him. There was a wall of silence surrounding the Milats, and there was no hope of the police breaking through it and getting the information they needed. Any one of them would have killed any other for the crime of betraying the family. There was no way that any of them would break under questioning given the tightness of their familial ties, so the police investigation more or less stalled out. They knew Ivan was responsible, but they couldn't prove it.

As a consequence of all the suspicion being levelled at Ivan, he and his family lived for a time in a sort of limbo, waiting to hear back on whether he would be charged for his crimes or whether he had slipped through the fingers of the law once more. It was a strange, liminal time between his usual bouts of endless activity. Observed constantly by the police, he could not do anything much, but neither could he lapse into stillness, as his nature would not allow it. Feeling the burden of the constant scrutiny of the police, the entire family was going stir-crazy working the farm and lingering around the house. Even their usual hunting trips into the outback had to be curtailed as a great many of the weapons that they owned weren't legal, strictly speaking. Should the police catch sight of them with these weapons, it could potentially result in charges being brought against them that were completely unrelated to the robberies that the police were hoping to pin on the family.

Ivan and his siblings took to aimless wandering, they took long drives, and they meandered casually about town. Anything to get them away from the house. They couldn't spend much money without attracting the attention of the police who were tailing their every move, so they mostly just loitered in public areas, doing nothing much at all.

Ivan himself took to walking the road near the family home, driving off the cops by his presence as they tried to remain unseen while he ambled up and down. Ivan's roaming often meant he was not home when his father came home. It afforded him some time away from the man, some privacy, some time alone with these thoughts.

It also meant that when his younger brother Wally was taking a drive with his little sister Margaret, Ivan saw them heading along that road back towards the house from whatever outing they'd been on. Without even realising it, he began to smile at the sight of his favourite little sister. Without even realising why, she started to smile back.

Which was about the moment that Wally drove head-on into an oncoming car.

They were both launched forward in the rickety old truck, the seatbelt locking in place for Wally on the driver's side but doing nothing at all for Margaret Junior. It spooled out and utterly failed to slow her as she was flung chest first into the dashboard, head snapping forward to crack spiderwebs into the glass.

Almost as horrifying as that first impact was the way that she was flung back again, her thin neck having snapped forward by the initial impact, now snapped back by the whiplash. The skin on her throat tore. Blood streamed down onto the blouse that Ivan had bought for her. She was so contorted that her forehead hit the headrest behind her. With another impact, her little body further mangled out of shape.

All while Ivan watched.

He broke into a run before the scream of tortured metal even reached him. Dashing across the road and past the car that had hit them without even a glance. He didn't care about them; they were strangers. He barely even spared a glance for Wally to make sure that he was breathing before he was trying to rip the crumpled door on Margaret's side open. It was mangled and twisted almost as badly as sweet little Margaret—lying there on the other side of the shattered safety glass—so crushed by the impact that nobody sane would have even attempted to get it open without the Jaws of Life or some other tools. Ivan was beyond panic, beyond grief, all the way across the horizon into whatever place it is that grants hysterical strength. Straining with all his hard-won might, he hauled the door to the car off its hinges and tossed it aside as if it were nothing.

Margaret was there, right in front of him. Her soft eyes closed as though she were only sleeping. Blood pooled around her neck. Her face was bruised up top where she'd hit the windshield and freckled with red where the tiniest fragments of glass had broken away to shower her. He'd seen her look worse after roughhousing with their sisters. She could walk away from this. Of course, she could. He took hold of her head where it lay limp and lank on the end of her neck, and he pulled it back up into place. Back to where it should be. She was going to be fine.

Just fine. She was sleeping. Just sleeping. Sometimes when you took a knock, it knocks you out. That was alright. That didn't mean anything.

He was saying her name, over and over, not yelling, even though he could feel the mounting horror climbing up his throat, but whispering it, nice and soft so that when she woke up it wouldn't startle her. The same way he'd woken her a hundred times. He placed gentle kisses on her cheeks, tasting the salt of blood on his lips when he was done. He pleaded with her to wake up. Please wake up. There were words never spoken in the Milat house. Things they only heard other families say or heard on the radio. He whispered those words to her now. He told her that he loved her, even though he couldn't know for sure what it meant. He whispered it and begged her, again and again, to wake up.

He was still cradling her body when the ambulance arrived, and it took all his brothers to haul him away from Margaret so that the paramedics could get in and do their work. Wally had long since stirred and crawled away from the wreckage.

Not one of them had ever seen Ivan cry. Not since they were babies. No matter what brutality their father had doled out, he had not shed a tear. No matter how he was beaten, abused, cursed at or threatened, nothing had ever broken through his cold outer shell. He had planned bank robberies without flinching, fought armed men to a standstill with his bare hands, and fed the whole family with nothing but a few bullets and his wits about him. Yet at this moment, he could not hide his weakness.

Of all the people in the world, Margaret Junior was the only one that he had ever truly loved. Every other relationship was poisoned by association with his father, by his wicked behaviour, everything except for Margaret. She was the apple of his eye. The one thing that he'd ever cared about. Even if the rumours of incest circulated in later years were not true, there can be no denying that she was his first and only love. The one anchor that kept him attached to the real world. And now she was gone.

Dead Inside

If Ivan's rage had been a fearful sight, so much worse was his grief.

At least when he had been angry, it could be directed. When one of them crossed him or made a mistake, he'd turn that energy into something productive. He'd plan a little harder, solve the problem, beat whoever was standing up to him senseless and then call that the end of it. But the death of Margaret left him changed in new, terrible, unforeseen ways. He had never smiled all that much before, but there had usually been some bitter amusement in his expression when he spent time with his family. Now it was as though he weren't there at all. Nothing went in, nothing came out. His head was lined with lead, and whatever thoughts were dwelling inside of it, nobody could ever know.

The precision that had marked so much of his criminal career began to slip as he lost his focus. When it came time for planning, he was still as sharp as ever, still maximising their odds of coming out of every situation as the winner, but in the moment, the killer instinct that had seen them through so many crises seemed to be blunted. It was as though he genuinely did not care what the outcome was.

With the tragedy that had rocked the family, the police pulled back their surveillance. Assuming quite rightly that there would be no more bank robberies while all the perpetrators were distraught. In this, they were correct.

Ivan was in a downward spiral. His other brothers and sisters could not pull him out of it, though they tried their best. His father saw his emotion as weakness but was around so rarely that it made little difference, and his mother was lost in her own grief over the loss of a child.

He took to travelling by night. When all his work was done but sleep would not come, he drove off along the backroads and the main, travelling just to travel, just to see the dark world zooming by, as though he could outrun his sorrow. Without sleep, his mind loosened even more. He became sluggish and mindless, completing his menial tasks with no flair or effort, only the relentless automatic motion of muscle memory.

It was the same when he was driving. He could not have said afterwards where he had been or what he had done, he was so numb that he might drive all the way across the continent and into the sea without realising it. Yet slowly, oh so slowly, little parts of who he had been began to re-emerge. His restlessness was reasserting itself. It hovered just beneath the surface, though it had been crushed by recent events, it was beginning to demand appeasement. All the paralytic stillness that came with his immense grief coupled with the stillness necessitated by so much police surveillance was beginning to catch up to him. And so, he drove and drove, trying to outpace the darkness on his heels and the prickling beneath his skin. That desperate need to *do something*.

Less than a month after his sister died in late 1971. He did something. Often when he was on his night-time rambles, he would see hitchhikers by the side of the road. Typically, he would ignore them, sometimes even treating them to a less than polite gesture if they were too close to the cars zipping by. But as the time dragged on, he began to find his eye drawn to any women out travelling at night. Muttering to himself about how unsafe it was, how they were just asking for trouble. Convincing himself that they were, in fact, deliberately putting themselves into a dangerous situation. A situation made all the more dangerous by his presence on the roads.

So far as we know, he never picked up any women out alone during that month, but when he saw a pair of them by the roadside outside of Liverpool, he pulled up alongside them and invited them inside, offering to take them to wherever they wanted to go. He had all night with nowhere to be, and he told them he was happy for the company. He even smiled at them, though close examination would have revealed that the smile never reached his eyes.

The girls felt safe because they outnumbered him, and though he was a large man, they didn't suspect that he'd try anything untoward with a witness in the car. They underestimated him at their peril.

Driving off along back roads which he told them were shortcuts, he led them out into the dark of the outback and then produced a knife and some rope. Using one as a hostage to keep the other from fleeing, he took his time tightly binding both of the girls in the backseat of the car. He then began to strip the two women, using his knife to part clothes from flesh where he had, to work around the bindings.

They struggled and screamed, but he stopped them dead with just a few words. 'You know what I'm gonna do? I'm going to kill you. Won't scream much if I cut your throats, will ya?'

With both girls naked, but for their nylon ropes, he seemed at a loss for a moment, but if they hoped it was an attack of conscience they would soon be let down. He had no conscience. All he had were two choices that he was too excited to pick between. Eventually, he just grabbed the girl that was closest and began raping her while the other watched on. Though they screamed and screamed at the top of their lungs, the noise could not carry far over the thrum of the engine. Not that it would have helped. There was not another living human being in earshot. He could stand out there in the outback firing his gun into the air and it wouldn't be heard or seen. They were so far out that if he had just left them there unbound, it still would have been murder.

Once he had taken his pleasure with the first victim, he found that he had lost all appetite for the other. He made some vague threats to them about keeping their mouths shut, cut their bindings, and then settled back into the front seat of his truck to continue their journey. As he drove, they wept and would not look at him. They fumbled their way back into their butchered clothes, trying their best to protect what little dignity they had left.

What would have followed next, whether they would have survived the night if everything had gone according to Ivan's plans, we will never know. He drove on along the motorway for a while in silence, eyes forward, as though he were alone in the car, and did his best to ignore the sobbing and the whimpering.

It began to grate on him before too long—too familiar, too like his little sister lying in her bed sobbing after one of the other boys had hurt her too badly. 'Pop. What say I buy you gals a bottle of pop?'

It was a childish trick to cheer them up, to stop the sobbing that had become so oppressive it made Ivan forget what he was doing. Nobody could cry and drink a silly fizzy drink at the same time. It would settle them down and then... then he could decide what he wanted to do next.

Pulling into the next petrol station, he finally turned off his truck, letting the night's silence wash back in, and toddled off to get them their drinks. The girls did not let the opportunity pass them by. As one, they slipped out of the cabin of the truck and ran for the cover of the nearby scrub bushes. Their hearts were pounding as they crouched there in pitch black, trying desperately to see what was happening without showing themselves. Trying desperately to hold together their ruined clothes.

Through the bushes they caught sight of Ivan coming out with their drinks. Saw him stop dead, staring into the back of his truck where they were meant to be. As though in slow motion, he turned slowly around to take in the surrounding area, tracing over the tarmac where they had scrambled and run as though he could see their tracks there, eyes locking on the scrub bush that they were huddled behind. Their breathing stopped. Their panic mounted. Maybe if they just came back quietly, they wouldn't be punished too badly. One of them started to rise, but the other, the one who had already suffered the feeling of Ivan forcing himself inside of her, caught her friend by the wrist and slowly shook her head. If it came to it, she would rather fight and die than ever again experience what Ivan considered lovemaking.

They stayed there in a kind of stand-off for a long moment, then Ivan appeared to shrug, climbed back into his truck and drove off.

He considered it to be a transaction fulfilled. They considered it to be the most brutal crime that they'd ever heard of, let alone experienced. As soon as he was out of sight they rushed into the petrol station, begging to use the phone, to call the police, telling broken fragments of what had happened to the confused cashier, who had seen nothing wrong with Ivan at all.

A police car was sent out to fetch them. The gas station clerk was interviewed for whatever details he could provide, and they headed directly to the nearest police station in the nearest town to file their complaint.

From the report that they gave, the description of the vehicle, and what the clerk had said, it took only minutes to identify Ivan Milat as the perpetrator. Rape was not his usual kind of crime, but the description that they gave of the truck and of him was too perfect a match for it to be anyone else. There was also the fact that he was already wanted in connection with a violent crime of a non-sexual nature. It painted a picture of a brutal thug who thought himself above repercussions, but not a particularly clever one given that he hadn't even attempted to hide his identity when abducting, raping, and then releasing two women. Not to mention allowing them to run free in such a foolish manner.

That was the only thing that gave the investigating officers pause. Here was a man that they believed could meticulously plan out a bank heist, yet he had somehow lost all sense when it came time to commit another crime.

The unfortunate women who had suffered in Ivan's tender care were questioned and requestioned again and again to try to make sense of it. And each time, their stories were a little different. It made the police suspicious; it made them think that this was some sort of setup. That these women were trying to get Ivan in trouble for some reason or another, or that they were even working with Ivan to try and manipulate his contact with the police and make them blow the slow surveillance operation that they'd been working up for so long. Instead of Ivan being immediately arrested for his well-documented crimes of kidnapping and rape, they delayed and dithered, trying to get their case together for the bank robbery, too, so that there would be no chance that evidence might be lost or manipulated.

After all, it wasn't as though a conniving criminal was suddenly going to stop caring about whether or not he got caught, was it? News of the police investigation reached Ivan's family through the grapevine, and from them, it passed to him in no time at all. With a rush of adrenaline, he realised the danger that he was in and actually felt alive again for the first time since Margaret's passing. For the first time since her funeral, he actually cared if he lived or died.

Gathering up what he could, he caught the next flight to New Zealand. By the time the police did come knocking, he was long gone and had already disappeared into the backcountry of the little green island to the east. Vanishing from sight before the local police could even be informed that he was there.

In the aftermath of this disappearing act, the Sydney police probed Ivan's family about his sudden disappearance, and they provided the almost unanimous statement that he had committed suicide in grief over the death of his sister. The method of suicide was not stated, and no body could be

provided but still, they stuck to their story, hoping to get the police off Ivan's back permanently. Perhaps if he had devised this particular plan, rather than his somewhat dimmer brothers, he might have managed to fabricate some evidence pointing in the direction of his death. Instead, the police simply made a few calls until they came upon the airline company that had sold Ivan his ticket and disregarded anything the Milats had to say, as per standard operating procedure when dealing with that family.

And so began Ivan's exile. Without his family, without his life. Alone in the world with nothing but a pocket full of stolen cash and whatever he could scrape together. His father might have had survivalist dreams of living off the land, but Ivan was in a state of true desperate survival, willing and able to do anything at all if it put a roof over his head and food in his belly.

There was no shortage of odd jobs in New Zealand for a man with his particular set of skills, and he actually lived in some degree of comfort, passed along from one farm to the next, herding sheep, laying bricks, doing whatever was required that nobody else was willing to do. If there was a job so dirty that even a farmer wouldn't touch it, Ivan was the one that they'd call. Every job, cash in hand. No questions asked.

For three years, he lived unseen. Off the radar, off the grid, completely unknown. Completely alone, too, with nothing but his thoughts for company. He could trust nobody fully because nobody was family. He couldn't even fake his way through a normal way of life for long because that same restless energy that had always driven him on to greater and greater things was still there. Roiling around just under the surface. Demanding that he act. That he head out into the dark and claim whatever he wanted.

Whether he was able to resist that call or not, we will never know. Little to no trace of him can be found in accounts from New Zealand. Even those passing glimpses that people had of him could be misidentifications. He was never arrested, never generated any sort of official paperwork, and barely seemed to even speak to anyone during those three years. He lived like a ghost for as long as he could until ultimately, he could bear his solitude no more. He had not written, and he had not called. He couldn't risk any communication being tracked back to him. He had been completely bereft of his whole family while he spent his years mourning the loss of his little sister.

Finally, it was too much. He took a flight back home.

He was identified before he even made it through the airport, but rather than intervening and having to transport him themselves, the New Zealand customs officers simply placed a phone call to the airport in Sydney and let Australia clean up their own mess. Ivan stepped off the plane and straight into police custody without a moment's delay, and from there it was a short stay in jail before he had his day in court.

Three years had passed since the bank robbery he was accused of committing, and the police were no closer to proving his guilt than they had been before he left. He stood trial for it, silently and sullenly, and when the prosecution could not provide ample evidence, the jury was forced to declare him not guilty. From there he went down to the courthouse cells to sleep through the night before being dragged before a new judge in the morning to face his rape charge.

The poor women who had been abducted had spent three years trying to forget what had happened to them. They had tried to move on. When the time came for them to tell their stories, their accounts did not even vaguely resemble the statements that they gave on the night that he had taken them, nor did they even vaguely resemble one another's. Trauma and time had muddled their memories to the point that the case essentially dissolved. The prosecutor was once again forced to throw the case to the whims of the jury and discovered that once more, they were willing to believe that the sad-eyed Milat who had been run off from his home and sent into exile was not responsible for whatever the women had been through—if it had been anything at all. In the eyes of most jurors, the two women had been asking for trouble hitchhiking in the dead of night. To them, as to Ivan on that awful night that he took them, it was the women who looked guilty.

Ivan's story was that the encounter had been entirely consensual and that he was sorry that they'd decided after the fact that they weren't willing to trade sex for a ride, but he couldn't undo what had been done.

One of the police officers who had been involved in the investigation was there in the courtroom, and he could hardly believe his eyes. He later described the case, saying that Ivan was the coolest man that he'd ever met. He went into the court as though he were entirely innocent of all wrongdoing and didn't even show a hint of the nervousness that usually afflicted even the innocent when they were faced with the possibility of imprisonment. Ivan met the gaze of the law head-on, and he did not flinch. It was a small wonder that the jurors found him to be entirely convincing.

In perspective, it made perfect sense. Why would Ivan, who had spent almost half a decade behind bars by this point, have any fear of it? To him, prison had always been like a holiday, a place where he got to experience some of the modern luxuries that the average Australian considered to be nothing special at all.

Television and toaster ovens. A bed in a room of his own. Three square meals a day. Everything about prison was an improvement over the way that he lived when he wasn't in the state's care, so what could frighten him about it? Some of the best friends he'd ever made had been on the inside, and some of the best tricks he'd learned had come from them.

For three years, Ivan had been in hiding, away from all that he cared about, for fear of punishment, and now that the time had come to face the music, he suffered nothing at all. Throughout his youth, he learned that his actions had consequences. If he transgressed, then he felt pain. After what he had done to those hitchhiker girls, he had expected outright torture, but all that he went through was the anxiety of fearing that punishment instead of anything more substantial. It shook his worldview to its core. If he could do whatever he pleased without fear of consequences, then why wouldn't he?

Ivan dedicated himself to a return to normal life now that he no longer had the threat of imprisonment hanging over him. Intent on giving all appearances of not having been changed at all by this experience, he went back to living with his parents, helping with their crops, and their home, and funnelling all his income to them. In addition to the ceaseless chores around the house, it did not take Ivan long to find a new job, driving long-haul transport trucks across Australia for days or even weeks at a time. The local police kept an eye on him for a time, but gradually they came to believe that the man who had returned from New Zealand was a reformed character. He was meticulously clean and tidy, he didn't smoke, he didn't drink, and he seemed to spend every waking moment supporting his gradually ageing parents. Whatever crimes he may have committed during his misspent youth it seemed that he was diligently making up for them now. In fact, the closest thing that Ivan seemed to have to a fault during the early seventies was that he was a workaholic. He took on every job that came along, working as hard as any two other men to prove himself, either to the company or to his father.

During this period of quiet, the Milat family suffered a series of equally quiet tragedies. While out riding on his motorbike, Ivan's brother David lost control of the machine and spun out across the motorway. Being the young rebel that he was, he had not elected to wear a helmet, and as a result, he was left with permanent debilitating brain damage that meant he had to return to living in the family home so that Margaret could take care of him.

If Ivan had been a workaholic before, then there was no word for what he became when returning to what had been his family home had to hear. The inhuman-sounding squawks and squeals that constantly escaped from David's lips, day and night. Ivan spent every waking moment working, and those moments that he couldn't, he spent in the outback hunting or driving along the motorways in his own vehicle. Anything was better than being home. Anything was better than hearing the cacophony of his own brother reduced to a mawkish shadow of the man that he had been.

He spent more and more time with his siblings when he couldn't work, dragging them away from the homes and families that they'd made in his absence to reminisce over the old times, or just to malinger around in isolated spots. Some of them would come out with him on his long late-night drives. Some would come shooting with him. None of them ever had the closeness that he'd shared with little Margaret, but some of his sisters began to come close. Shirley Soire (neé Milat) was probably the closest thing that he had to a friend in those days, willing and able to drop everything in her newly married life to go hang out with her cool big brother that she'd never been able to get the time of day from before. They drove around in the dead of night for hours when they both should have been sleeping, her in bed with her husband, and Ivan in his bunkbed above David.

There was no question that Ivan was still the 'alpha' of this little pack, but as everyone matured so too did the relationships. They were able to communicate with one another and act like actual siblings rather than fighting for dominance all the time. They began to become friends as well as survivors of Stjepan's enforced childhood from hell.

With the perspective that age and distance brought, the Milat kids began to see just how bizarre and harsh their upbringing had been, and that realization drove a wedge between them and their father at the most inopportune of times. Inopportune because some of the groaning and screaming echoing through the Milat house was not coming from David, but from their father.

Bowel cancer was probably not the dignified way in which he had hoped to go. Squirming and groaning as it felt like his intestines had turned into millipedes, writhing and biting and burning with venom inside of him. He withered before the eyes of his wife and children. Shrinking in on himself day by day like fruit left out in the sun.

The old man had been a tyrant his entire life. Working the whole family to the bone and enforcing his will by virtue of his strength. But like every tyrant, when robbed of his ability to rule by violence, he rapidly lost his grip.

As he lost control over his children, they began to depart. No longer did they show up obediently at his barked command to cook and clean and farm. No longer did all the money that those children earned flow into a communal coffer.

As Stjepan became too sick to work at the docks, Ivan's income was now the only money coming into the household to care for both his parents and his permanently disabled brother. He worked and he worked, and not a penny ever went into his pocket. This drove a wedge between Ivan and the rest of his immediate family. He came to resent them for the freedom that they'd won by ignoring the call. Here he was, spending all day and night working to keep the family together, to keep a roof over their heads, and everyone else had just left without even asking his permission.

As Stjepan's health grew ever worse, so too did his attitude. He lashed out constantly at everyone around him, but Ivan, as the only one who was fully competent, seemed to suffer the worst of it. He was still young and strong, all the things that Stjepan wished to be, and Stjepan loathed him for it. Day and night he rained insults down on Ivan, and like the dutiful son that he was, Ivan simply endured. Taking that hatred, turning around, and spitting it out again in every direction.

The close bonds that enduring their father's torments had gifted the Milat children seemed to come apart when he was no longer there as a common enemy to unify them. There was no longer any need to present a united front. There was no more need for them to be a family anymore, as many of them saw it.

Given that the majority of Ivan's social circles were simply his siblings and their respective families, this created even more of a problem for him than could be expected. He ended up spending his time with cousins on his mother's side. People he considered to be soft and weak, city folk who were beneath contempt. Yet here he was following after them just for the sake of having some company.

Stjepan Milat died on the 27th of April 1983, at the age of 81 and was buried in a Catholic ceremony at Rookwood Cemetery alongside his daughter Margaret. The funeral was attended by his wife and only two of his children, Ivan and David.

The three of them returned to the family home afterwards to host something vaguely resembling a reception but with none of the joviality that drives such an event. Few of the guests lingered long, and fewer still had anything nice to say about the dearly departed. They were there to offer sympathy and kindness to Margaret senior, not to pretend that Ivan was anything other than a festering wound of rage.

In the aftermath of Stjepan's death, there was a small insurance payout and pension that ensured that the house would continue to be paid for and that Margaret would not struggle. Ivan took this as a sign that his duty was finally done and that his own life could finally begin. He left behind his mother and David, who had now lapsed into blessed near-perpetual silence, and he set out to start over again.

A Normal Life

With his sister's memory slowly fading and his father no longer leering over his shoulder, Ivan felt that it was finally time for him to take a wife and settle into a life of his own. He had no shortage of money, thanks to the frugal life that he had always lived, and he soon purchased a caravan for himself to live in and parked it out in the garden of one of his extended family members who wasn't too fussy about his comings and goings.

In addition to the change in location, Ivan also sought out a change in job. Driving a truck was all fine and good, but that itchy feeling under his skin didn't get any better without activity. Hard labour. He needed it like others needed food. To feel his muscles working. To feel alive. Still, he had racked up so many hours on the road that he hardly wanted to abandon all the skill he'd developed there. Few people could drive as long and hard as Ivan Milat, and when he announced that he was no longer going to be driving lorries around, it was a real blow to his company. For a time, he bounced from job to job, holding five of them in five different places over the course of a year. Every single employer was sorry to see him go when he left on his own terms to pursue the next one. He wasn't just a hard worker, he was relentless. He was a machine. He put all their other employees to shame with how dutifully he undertook his tasks. Yet none of these jobs ever quite managed to scratch the itch. Something physical and on the road. Something where the strength of his body and his ability to drive forever and ever were intermingled so that he would never feel bored, restless, and out of place.

He found a new job out on the roads that would still let him out to stretch and work with his hands as he craved. A job with the New South Wales Road and Traffic Authority, travelling the motorways and back roads that he knew so well, examining them for damage and conducting repairs and refurbishments. Sometimes he would be travelling alone, sometimes he'd be working with his currently estranged brother Richard on a road gang. It wouldn't be until later, when the hard feelings had abated, that he'd discover that the only reason he got offered the job was that his brother had vouched for him so vociferously. Even if they were fighting right then, they were still family.

Still feeling that lack of family, Ivan was spending yet more time with his cousins, and while most of them were not of any great interest to him, one of them had something that was of great interest to him. Karen was the girlfriend of one of his younger cousins. While Ivan had dalliances with relationships in the past, they all fizzled out soon after his lust was fulfilled. With Karen, it was a different story entirely. He saw her, and he wanted her, but he was denied.

Her relationship with his cousin was not one of the casual dalliances that Ivan was accustomed to. The two of them had been together for months. There were talks of marriage. Talks which had accelerated rapidly when she began to show a baby bump. She wasn't just forbidden to him because she belonged to another man, or because it would upset his family. She was forbidden because she was pregnant with another man's child. It was so taboo nobody would have even considered the possibility even if they would have considered pursuing a relationship with a sixteen-year-old girl when they were a grown adult. But Ivan didn't just consider it, he was obsessed with it. At every opportunity, he would spend time with her at family gatherings. While her boyfriend was off working, Ivan would show up to help her with things around the house that she could have managed just fine given how early she was in the pregnancy but that he insisted were too strenuous for her.

The fact that she wasn't immediately available to him meant that he couldn't just charm his way into her pants and be done with it. For the first time, he was forced to spend extended amounts of time with a woman, talking with her as though she was a person instead of a prize to be claimed. He spoke to her honestly about his life and listened when she spoke about hers. All of the things that normal people did when they were trying to develop a relationship, he did by accident. All of the kindness that he showed her as an excuse to hang around her, also accidental, but nonetheless effective. While he was stalking her like prey, she was falling in love with him.

At some point before she was too far along into her pregnancy, they consummated their blossoming relationship, and while that would usually have been the end of things for Ivan, this time he still felt the same draw that had brought him to her doorstep time and time again.

There is a trend when describing violent criminals to act as though they are incapable of feeling love or any of the emotions that we describe as being positive. That they are emotionally stunted in ways that prevent them from functioning like normal people, and this is the source of their criminality. A modern interpretation of the old idea that some people are simply born evil. But once again, Ivan proved himself not only capable of love but completely consumed by it. Almost as soon as their relationship had progressed beyond the batting of eyelashes to something more significant, he was already laying out plans for their future together. Before she even announced to his cousin that she was going to be leaving him, Ivan already had his mobile home set up for her, ready to provide whatever she might need throughout her pregnancy. His thriftiness and workaholic tendencies had left him with a not-insubstantial amount of money, and he was more than willing to spend it on his beloved girlfriend. Everything was made perfect for her before he'd even asked her if she would consent to move in with him.

As should have been expected, this was about the time that the shit hit the fan with the family.

His cousin was understandably furious to learn that the girlfriend that he'd knocked up was now sleeping with Ivan. His parents and all of the collective relatives on his mother's side were horrified by this turn of events, at least at first. To them, Ivan's cousin and Karen having a baby together was already bad news—he was a young man with no prospects to speak of, and he had essentially condemned himself, her, and the baby to a lifetime of poverty by his decisions. The family was already resigned to the inescapable conclusion that they'd be the ones called upon to pick up the slack, to help out with the baby when the young lovers proved themselves inadequate to the task of supporting a child, and to pick up the tab for all the innumerable costs that were going to be involved. But now, thanks to Ivan's unseemly intervention, they were essentially absolved of that duty. They could just treat the pair of them as pariahs and never have to deal with the embarrassing and expensive burden of the bastard child.

At least, that was their intention at first. But it was only days after Ivan had taken Karen into his home that the new couple announced their engagement. That was when they learned that Ivan intended to care for her and the baby as though they were his own, they realised that this was not some flight of fancy on his part but maybe something resembling love. All of them remembered his gentleness when it came to his little sisters, the way that he had doted on and cared for Margaret in particular. To their surprise, it soon became apparent that Ivan was the better choice to be with her. In their world full of struggle and strife, this man who had a career, a home of his own, and all the skills it would take to support himself and others was the more mature and sensible option for Karen. This realisation likely came as much of a shock to them as it did to Ivan, himself. He may have been the wild child of one of their cousins, raised by some old foreign madman, but despite that fact, he was still a better provider and father than anyone could have hoped.

Karen and Ivan were wed in 1985. None of his immediate family were in attendance due to the ongoing feud between all the siblings over responsibility for the care of their now-dead father. None of the cousins that he had replaced them with could attend either, not without exacerbating the divide that had been wedged into the family as the result of his running off with his little cousin's girl. But at the same time, the absence did not seem to sting Ivan too badly. His own stance towards his siblings was softer now, softened further by the adoration and kindness that he'd found in Karen.

Before Ivan's adoptive son even came into the world, all of his aunts and uncles were back in the picture, old wrongs forgiven if not forgotten. Ivan's entire social circle re-formed around him, encircling him and Karen and isolating them both from the world in the same way that they always had. Karen was part of the family now, and that came with a degree of obligation to remain loyal to the family. To keep their secrets, to live among them, to make her world only as large as they were comfortable with. On the one hand, it was smothering, on the other, it was the kind of embrace that nobody could have expected when marrying into a new family, particularly under the rather awkward circumstances that she had to navigate.

Her son Jason was born before they could be married, and while Karen, and everyone else, had fully expected Ivan to be as standoffish as his own father when it came to babies, the situation could not have been more different. He cared for that baby as though it was his own. Even going to the trouble of filing the papers to legally adopt the boy when the opportunity arose. When the night-time feedings came around, he was up and out of bed like a shot. When the baby wouldn't settle, he'd strap it into its car seat in his truck and take little Jason for a silent drive through the darkness until he was out like a light. It might have seemed that there was no room in Ivan's perfectly ordered life for a mewling baby, but it seemed to complete him.

Yet as much as he cherished his time with Jason and Karen, the same workaholic compulsion still drove him out the door to work all the hours that were sent his way. He was away for days at a time, leaving Karen oddly bereft, as though she were a single mother. And while he was always kind and understanding with

Jason, Ivan still had standards of cleanliness and organisation that he wanted to be maintained in his home. At first, these standards were presented politely and plainly—an explanation of what needed to be done to keep standards up while he was out at work. Nothing too strenuous. Nothing that he didn't think he could achieve given the same timeframe. Certainly, nothing that he wouldn't handle himself if he came back to find the place a mess.

Karen missed him when he was gone, but at least she had Jason for company. He wasn't much of a conversationalist, but if she did want to talk, she'd have one of the many Milat siblings swinging by to check on her almost daily anyway. Dropping in food, sharing advice, and just hanging around to make sure she felt taken care of. She'd never heard Ivan ask any of them to do any of this, and they didn't seem to do it for any of the other members of the family, so far as she could tell. She wasn't sure if she was under surveillance, or if they all just worshipped Ivan so much that they were willing to go out of their way to try and stay in his good books.

When she tried to bring it up with him, he was confused. He'd done the same for all of them when he could when he wasn't busy taking care of their mother, or their disabled brother, or a million other little problems for them. It was just the way that his family was. Close and caring and entirely involved in everyone else's business to a degree that felt grossly invasive to Karen.

Of course, she couldn't complain. Not when a brother showed up out of the blue to rake the leaves, or a sister dropped in with a casserole for their dinner. It might have been overwhelming, but it was never sinister. It was nice, just... too much.

Ivan's work took him away for weeks at a time, travelling the highways and byways of New South Wales, working and moving on, sleeping in the cabin of his truck, or under the stars by night, and then starting all over again. He worked longer hours and did harder work than anyone else on the Main Roads team, never hesitating to volunteer for more. He had a reason now. A justification to always be busy, away from his wife and child. They were saving up enough money to put a deposit down on a house.

It was the light at the end of the tunnel, the pot of gold at the end of the rainbow. All their problems would be solved once they were out of the cramped confines of the caravan. He wouldn't need to work all hours once they had a house, so he'd be around. There would be more space so all of his stuff, her stuff, and things for the baby wouldn't be piled up, making things look messy and upsetting Ivan when he got home. He could go back to being the sweet caring man that she had fallen in love with instead of what he was becoming.

Ivan had always been frugal. It was how he had so much in the way of savings to begin with, but now that their courtship was over and Karen was settled into the mobile home, he seemed unwilling to part from a single penny. When the baby needed new clothes, he would gripe that they'd only just bought him new ones the month before. When they needed food, he'd gripe that they were eating too much and that they should really get a garden going to provide for them. Not that he ever had time to farm, even if there was somewhere they could do so. Whatever tiny expense Karen and the baby faced, he seemed to resent paying for, as though the house in his mind was the only thing that mattered and all else was just a distraction.

While Karen had flourished under his undivided attention, she now seemed to wither as that attention was entirely withdrawn. He worked, and he worked, and he worked. Vanishing for days, sometimes weeks at a time before sauntering back in as though he'd just stepped out for a pack of cigarettes. His family continued to visit, but she increasingly suspected that they were jailors as much as visitors, checking in to make sure that she didn't roam too far without his eyes on her. Even with their eyes on her, there seemed to be a thread of paranoia strung through all her conversations with Ivan now, as though he suspected infidelity even though there was no possibility of her even having a moment to herself with a baby to care for and his exacting standards of cleanliness, let alone the time to conduct some sort of love affair. Perhaps that seed of doubt was something like a conscience niggling away in Ivan's mind, reminding him that he had swept in and stolen her from someone else. When he was a little boy, competing with all of his brothers and sisters, nothing had ever truly belonged to him, or any of them. Possession was the rule of the day, whoever could take by force or steal something became its rightful owner, and only the threat of his violence ever kept the things that he was attached to in his possession.

Yet despite this dark edge to their interactions, she found her heart melting time and again when she saw him with the baby. When he was home, there were no night feedings for her. At the first faintest stirring of the baby, Ivan was up and in action, cradling the tiny form to his broad bare chest, the light of the open refrigerator the only illumination in the mobile home as he set about making up a bottle and feeding the baby, gently rocking it all the way to keep the quiet and let Karen sleep.

This dichotomy strung her along. The soft gentle and loving man that she knew he could be, and the cold, almost brutal creature he seemed to become when the sun rose and the road called to him. She assured herself that it was just stress, that he was doubtless exhausted from all the work that he was doing to support them, to build a better future for them. He was under pressure, and she was going to be the recipient of whatever steam he inadvertently let off. The fact that he was clamping down so hard on whatever was boiling up inside of him was clearly a sign that he was a good man, that he was making sure none of the exhaustion or anger could wash out onto their baby. And in the end, all of his hard work paid dividends. All of the odd jobs he'd picked up, all of the overtime, every penny that he pinched—leaving her to lie in bed at night with an empty stomach and his old ragged hand-me-down clothes because he wouldn't let her buy any of her own—it was all worthwhile in the end because by the time that little Jason was a little over a year old, Ivan announced that he was going to look at some houses.

Maybe Karen would have liked to be involved in the process a little more. Perhaps having a say in where she was going to be living for the rest of her married life would have been nice, but at the same time, she knew that she had contributed nothing to their marriage financially. It was all his money that he planned to spend on the house, so what right did she really have to tell him how it should be spent?

In the end, they moved into a two-bedroom house on Cinnibar Street, still in the rough rural suburbs of Sydney, this time one called Eagle Vale, far to the southeast of the city—now fairly well on its way to being fully domesticated but back then, exactly the sort of place that Ivan had grown up, right on the edge of wild country. Whatever flaws it might have had in terms of size or isolation from her friends and family, Karen set them aside, because she knew that now, finally, Ivan was going to change back. He was going to work normal hours and spend money like a normal person, and they were going to live a normal life, as he'd implicitly promised her back when he got down on one knee and asked her to be his wife. There was the stress of moving to navigate, of course. Then the trouble of selling off the mobile home. Then the irritation of having to go back and help out when his disabled brother took a bad turn and needed more help than his mother could offer. Just little normal things that were a part of life, but that kept him edgy. Kept him from easing back into being the man that she'd fallen in love with. Then there was the mortgage to contend with, of course. Buying a house wasn't cheap, and they'd still need to live frugally, at least for a while, until they were over the hump of all the moving costs and the expenses of furnishing the place. Though on reflection, Karen couldn't say what they actually had to pay for since the whole Milat clan seemed to show up carting trailers full of hand-me-down furniture and did almost every part of the refurbishment and redecoration of the house themselves.

He was still working all the time, but at least now she had some space to breathe. Jason had a room of his own, they had a garden for him to play in. She had an actual kitchen to cook the meals that sat cold and waiting for Ivan to come home. Everything was definitely better. Everything except for the one thing that she actually needed to change.

When he came home to her after days away, now there were arguments. Her spending was out of control. They didn't need to heat the whole house, only the rooms that they were in. Why did she need so many different sets of clothes when he'd paid good money for a washing machine? His childhood in an immigrant family ruled over by a man who was—if we are honest—not entirely sane, had set these impossibly high standards of penny-pinching. Even now when they had the deposit on their house down and everything was comfortably covered, he resented every dollar they spent.

Or rather, every dollar that Karen spent. With the purchase of the home completed, Ivan went back to many of his old hobbies once more without informing her. While she was struggling with the pittance that he gave her to make ends meet, he was off chatting with fellow hobbyists and enthusiasts, meeting up with collectors and making purchases to expand his own ever-growing collection. At no point did he consider his purchases to be unnecessary or consider the friction that it was going to cause with his wife. At least until Karen would be cleaning the house and come across yet another gun.

The first time that she found a gun in the house, she froze like a startled rabbit and just stared. She was not from the same background as Ivan, she did not understand that these things could be tools to serve a specific function. All that she knew of guns was from television. War, murder, violence. She knew in the abstract that he and his family hunted for meat in the same way that they tried to be self-sufficient by growing their own crops, but the reality now facing her still filled her with fear. She had a little boy in the house. A little boy already picking up sticks and running around making banging noises like he was shooting at people.

It took her longer than she liked to admit to work up the courage to touch the evil thing, and even when she had it in her shaking hands, she had no idea what to do with it. In truth, she wanted to run outside and throw it away with as much force as she could muster. She wanted to call the police and tell them that this omen of death had just appeared in her house and she needed them to come take it away. But she couldn't. She knew it belonged to her husband, and she knew that if it were to go missing, his wrath would be an awful thing to behold. She had to put it away somewhere. Somewhere that little hands couldn't reach it and inquisitive minds couldn't figure out how it worked. In the end, she settled for pushing it up on top of the wardrobe, leaving it in plain sight and keeping her perpetually on edge whenever she was in her bedroom, but also putting it far enough away that Jason wouldn't be able to touch it.

It was days later that Ivan returned home from work and she confronted him about it. He didn't understand the problem. Not in the sense that he was being deliberately ignorant to her concerns—he genuinely had not ever considered the possibility that having guns around the house might be a danger to Jason. The moment that he grasped that it was not normal for boys that were barely able to walk to be handling guns, he made no apology but was spurned into action. He gathered his various guns from where he'd hidden them around the house and bought a locker to stow them all away in safely.

She was happy about that. She had to be happy about that. She'd raised a concern and he'd taken her seriously and handled it, just like he was meant to, but having him wandering around the house plucking lethal weapons out of hidey holes she didn't even know existed had taken her breath away. There were so many of them. All these different makes and models, allegedly for hunting different prey, though she couldn't tell how it would make the slightest bit of difference which of the rifles, shotguns, handguns, or assault weapons he pointed at an animal when they all killed just the same. Some of them were antiques. Hand-me-downs from his father and beyond, from as far back as

World War 1. Others were strange-looking things that had come from other places all around the world. When she could bring herself to ask about them, he turned almost boyish again, gushing about which weapon was from where, what its specifications were, and the animals that he'd taken down with each one. Some were clearly meant to just be display pieces, but he kept them all oiled and functional as if he were about to go out and wage a one-man war tomorrow all by himself. She'd always known that she was sheltered compared to Ivan, that he'd lived a far harder and more violent life, but even with that in mind, she couldn't conceive of a world in which all these armaments were necessary. Yet Ivan didn't treat them with solemnity. He acted as though every one of them was a special toy, just for him. He delighted in them.

When she asked him to get rid of the guns, he point-blank refused. They were his. He gave her dominion over everything else in the house. Prettied it up for her however she liked. Paid for everything that she could think of to buy. There wasn't a chance in hell that he would dispense with the one thing in that house that he actually cared about, his prized cache of weapons. Not when he needed them to protect his home and to hunt for their dinner.

Until that moment, even though they had often argued, Ivan had never brought up their disparity in age and experience. This could be because he genuinely did not recognise it as a factor in their relationship, or more likely because he did not wish to draw attention to the fact that he had pursued a relationship with someone so much younger than himself. Also, it was entirely possible that he was trying to put the difference in their age out of his own mind so that he would not have to acknowledge that the girl he had relentlessly pursued and now worked out all his sexual appetites on was exactly the same age as his little sister would have been had she not died in that horrific car accident right in front of him. Regardless, it was the card that he finally played when putting his foot down with Karen during this argument. She did not know what the world was like out there. She only knew the comfortable coddled life of a little girl. She had never had to kill or go hungry. She had never had to defend herself against a man who would kill her just as soon as look at her. She had not lived through the things that Ivan considered to be the formative moments in a person's life, so her opinion was not valid. He considered the guns to be not only a vital part of his life but also a source of great comfort. To know that no matter what might happen down the line, he would have the tools necessary to protect himself, protect Karen, and protect the son that they were raising together.

He never realised it, but it was that final dip into the sentiment that actually silenced Karen's arguments. She had seen only the danger to Jason in having all these guns around the house, but never the protection that they might offer. Ivan had locked them all away for safety, just like she'd asked, and he would only bring them out if he needed to, for hunting or protection of their home. How could she really begrudge him that? Still, she insisted that he had far too many of them. The man only had two hands, after all.

She wasn't going to force him to get rid of any, but she put a blanket ban on buying any more. Finally, Ivan seemed to understand her, making his apologies, embracing her, and promising that he'd stop spending money on guns. It was the money that he thought she was upset about. Even after days of arguing, he couldn't parse that there were people in the world who considered a gun to be an inherently bad thing. He made a note to himself to keep all future purchases hidden away from her and then moved on.

This was the first time that an argument had really gone against Ivan in any way. The first time that his young wife had the courage to hold her ground. Sure, neither of them had actually gotten exactly what they wanted, but that was nothing new for Karen. It was, however, a fresh and unwelcome sensation for Ivan, who was accustomed to his rule being unchallenged and absolute. It stung and he didn't like it one bit. It made him all the more argumentative when it came to any other issue. He became even more resolute that he must enforce his will in all other matters lest he lose control of his wife.

Meanwhile, it had instilled a fresh fight in Karen. She had stood up for herself and her son, and the world had not ended. Ivan hadn't torn down the sky or thrown a tantrum. It had taken some work to get through to him, but in the end, she felt like she really had, and that they both understood each other better now. She considered it to be a positive development in their relationship rather than a red flag. So, the next time that Ivan came storming in complaining about how something wasn't cleaned up to the standard that he expected, Karen stood her ground. She told him he was being unreasonable, that she had a small child to care for, and that she couldn't have every single thing in the house pristine every moment of every day. She'd get to every job as soon as she had the time, but she was busy, too.

He hit her.

It wasn't hard, not nearly as hard as it could have been given his strength, but it still shocked her into silence. She had always known that he was a rough man, but he'd never shown that aspect of his personality to her or Jason. He'd never hurt her before. Sworn blind that he never would. She couldn't believe that he'd raise a hand to her. Even lying there on the kitchen floor with her ears ringing, she couldn't believe it. Ivan looked shocked too. He mumbled his way through an apology, helped her back up, and went pale as though he were going to be sick. He had never meant to hit her, he said, never meant to hurt her. She truly believed that by the time he was done talking.

He went away after that, allegedly for work, but as far as Karen could tell, his work in those days mostly seemed to be driving around in the middle of nowhere so he could have some time alone to think. When he came back, he was still apologetic, so pathetic about it that Karen couldn't help but accept his apology and welcome him back into her waiting arms.

This set the precedent for the remainder of their marriage.

They would argue, often over a trivial matter, and when the argument started to go against Ivan, he would lash out physically. Never a punch or a kick like his father used to dole out, but a slap, or a push. Dragging her around by her hair. Little cruelties.

Still, she would not back down from him. To back down now would invalidate all that she'd already suffered for every tiny victory that she won. Ivan, so used to having his way, did not know how to back down either. He took every question as a challenge, every comment as the first shot fired.

The relatively gentle cycle that they'd first fallen into, where he'd lash out, apologise, and then give in to Karen's demands, began to erode away. He blamed her for deliberately making him angry so that he'd hit her, and she'd get what she wanted. More importantly, he gradually realised that she wasn't going to take flight every time that he struck her. The violence went from occasional, in the heat of the moment, to regular. The beatings went from openhanded slaps to closed-fist punches.

Needless to say, neither one of them was happy in the relationship anymore. Yet, just as neither of them could back down from an argument with one another, neither could either of them see any way out of the situation. Ivan was in no way capable of gracefully tolerating the loss of face with his family should his marriage fall apart, and Karen had lost any familial support system from her own friends and family as a result of the deliberate isolation imposed on her by her husband. To make matters worse, she was still under sporadic surveillance by Ivan's family. If she confided in any of them what had been going on, she had little hope that they'd help her. None of them would choose an outsider over their brother, and of all the brothers that she could have married, it was clear that Ivan was the one people were least willing to cross.

Ivan, on the other hand, had plentiful outlets to blow off steam. Now that he no longer felt beholden to Karen, or afraid that she might abandon him, he was free to behave exactly as he pleased. He escalated his purchases of firearms to include fully automatic weapons that should strictly have been available only to the military and took to hiding them around the house once more in special hand-crafted secret compartments he built solely for his own personal use. Karen thought that he'd gone 'gun crazy' and told him so, only to receive a backhand to the jaw for her trouble.

For obvious reasons, the romantic aspects of their marriage fell into disrepair. The gentle and kind man that she thought she'd married had been entirely subsumed back into the macho wild man person that Ivan showed to the rest of the world. He still maintained his old levels of kindness when it came to their son, but even that had begun to corrupt into a repetition of his own upbringing. He'd take Jason out hunting with him, and each time that the boy came home, he seemed to be less himself and more Ivan.

Without an outlet for his sexual energies, Ivan's eyes soon turned to the other women in his life that he considered to be readily available to him, eventually starting off a fitful affair with his brother Wally's wife, Maureen.

There were rumours at the time that he was involved, in a similar way, with many of his brothers' wives. That as the ruler of the Milat clan, he felt like he was entitled to sleep with whomever he pleased. There certainly didn't seem to be any fallout from his affair with Maureen that could be observed from the outside, but given how insular the family were, that proved very little. It was possible, of course, that Wally, or 'Walter', as he was known outside of the family, had no awareness of what was happening under his own roof, but given how pervasively the rumours of the affair circulated, it seems extremely unlikely. This would seem to indicate that either he knew of the rumours but, despite all evidence to the contrary, chose to take Ivan at his word, or that he knew of the affair, yet managed to crush his own feelings of betrayal and jealousy because crossing his brother was more dangerous than giving the man free reign to do as he pleased and allow the free use of his wife. Another alternative might be that he knew of the affair but simply did not care.

Karen heard all the whispers, of course. The other wives of the Milat brothers, and even Ivan's sisters, would sometimes drop in to gossip, and it seemed that there was no real effort being taken to cover things up. When she confronted Ivan about his infidelity, he responded in a typically violent manner. If she had been the one stepping out on him, then there would likely have been a murder, but because the positions were reversed, she was powerless to do anything at all. She had to endure silently and stoically, for Jason's sake as much as her own.

For years, she endured his coldness, his long unexplained absences, his penny-pinching, his violence, and his infidelity. She endured them in complete silence. Completely alone in the world. She bided her time until she just couldn't stand it anymore, and then she left him.

On Valentine's Day of 1987, Ivan returned home from work to discover that his wife was gone, his son was gone, and all the furniture in the house had vanished too. Through the hours that he was away, Karen's mother had arrived with a big pickup truck, and they had divested the house of absolutely everything. Everything except for Ivan's guns.

The point of contention that had started their slow drift away from one another was all that he had left now. His guns had mattered to him so much, and now he had nothing else.

He did not dare try to track Karen down. Not now that she was free to speak as she wished and could tell the sorry tale of how he'd been treating her the past few years. He had loved her with such passion as he had never before known, and now he found that he hated her with that very same passion.

Scrimping and saving, he slowly refilled his house with furnishings, though obviously not up to the liveable standard that Karen had insisted on. When the divorce papers came through, he fought tooth and nail to keep from having to give Karen and the brat a single penny after all that he'd done for them and all they'd taken from him. Jason, whom he had raised like his own son, had made no attempt to contact Ivan. It was as though all his efforts to turn the boy into a man who could stand on his own two feet were just poured down the drain. The fact that the boy was a little over two years old at that point was not relevant to Ivan. He had been capable of absolutely anything from the day that he was born, and that kid had been raised by him to be just as capable. Sure, he was still wobbly on his feet sometimes, but he must have been able to manage to place a simple call.

Karen was a bitch, a harridan, a nightmare succubus, he'd never trust her again after she abandoned him like this, and that made her a monster in his mind. But Jason, Jason had been his boy, his friend, he had hoped that meant something. But it seemed that the sentiment was not mutual. Jason stood by his mother and spoke not a single word out of turn.

Ivan and Karen never saw each other in person throughout the court proceedings. Her status as a battered wife was known, and the Australian justice system would not force her to stand in front of the man who had beaten her bloody day after day just so that she could demand what was due to her.

Despite impassioned pleas on the part of Ivan, denying all wrongdoing and clearly distraught over the whole thing, the law came down on Karen's side, and if Ivan attempted to circumvent the alimony that he was ordered to pay to her, they would simply garnish his wages to ensure that she was able to go on living off the sweat of his brow while he slept on a mattress on the floor and sat in lawn furniture in his living room.

And the worst part of it all was, he would have paid up readily. He would have given her and Jason everything that he had if they'd just asked him face to face. They were his family, his wife, and his son. They belonged to him, and they'd been snatched away without a word.

Even one phone call from Jason could have put everything right. Just one call, to say that he didn't blame his dad, and it was that miserable hell bitch who was responsible for ruining their lives.

That was all Ivan would have needed, and he'd have paid every penny of alimony to make sure that his boy was well taken care of. But that call never came. No visit or letter, either. It was as though they'd vanished off the face of the earth.

No. Not them. Ivan.

It was as though he'd vanished. As if he'd stepped on a crack and fallen into some awful bottomless abyss with no chance of climbing out, some underworld where everything looked basically the same, but was grey and miserable. They were everything to him. Everything. And now they were gone. It was enough to drive a man mad.

Breaking Point

Two years after he was abandoned by his wife, Ivan changed. The diligent, hard-working employee of the state roads department was gone, and in its place stood someone else entirely. Realising that the courts were indeed more than willing to garnish his wages to pay his ex-wife what she was owed, Ivan deliberately made himself unemployed to avoid having to pay her a penny.

For a workaholic such as Ivan, the idea of sitting around doing nothing all day, even out of spite, was unthinkable, so despite legally being considered unemployed, he managed to fill almost every day with one odd job or another for which he would be paid in cash, under the table. There was no shortage of odd jobs in rural areas that required a strong man with his head screwed on right, and with all his years of experience, both at home and in New Zealand, taking care of every problem that might arise, Ivan had constructed quite a resume for himself. Through the social network of his innumerable siblings and their friends and relatives, he was constantly being called on to help out with some joinery here, or someday-labouring there.

Of course, work in this legal grey area was not the only thing to occupy Ivan's time or to fill his pockets with cash.

While he was a married man, he was settled, with everything to lose if he was found to have broken the law. Now that Karen and Jason were gone, it was as though his leash had been cut and he was free to run wild again. He began picking up hitchhikers as he trawled up and down the motorways by night, alone in the silence with his thoughts, and those that he deemed to be wealthy enough, he robbed before dumping them at the nearest sign of civilisation.

He was a large and frightening man with a gun. Extorting the wallets and purses from terrified teenagers was hardly a challenge to him. More important than the money that he got from his crime spree was the power that he felt. Karen had robbed him of all his power when she'd abandoned him. She'd made him feel like he was less than a man. She'd made him feel guilty for the things that he knew had to have been the right thing to do because he was the one who had done them. He'd done them, and he was always the smartest guy in the room, so obviously, the choices he'd made were the best ones. It was without question. Yet she'd wormed her way into his head and made him feel like he was doing wrong. Then to make matters worse, the damn hand-wringing namby-pamby government had come along and told him that she was right! That he had done wrong. That a man had no right to discipline his wife when she talked back.

The divorce was finalised in 1989. That served as the final nail in the coffin of the decent family man that Ivan had been trying to be. An official stamp to officially certify his utter failure to achieve what his father had managed seemingly effortlessly. The old man was dead and gone, but Ivan had spent so long trying to claw his way out of his shadow that he didn't know how to do anything else. Losing his wife, his son, and his version of a family, hammered home to him that no matter how clever or strong or commanding he was, he'd never be a better man than old Stjepan.

Everything that had made Ivan human was gone now. Every connection he had to the normal world was severed. His days were spent labouring mindlessly, his nights roaming the highways outside of Sydney looking for hitchhikers to prey upon. Day and night began to blur together. He missed days of work to go driving around aimlessly. He'd show up to work hours after everyone else and then try to put in the same hours, working into the dead of night. Time itself had lost all meaning to him.

About a decade before all of this, the very first ConFest was organised by former Deputy Prime Minister Dr Jim Cairns. It was a bush campout festival meant to celebrate all of the various subcultures that made up Australia and was held yearly from that point on, generally falling around the time of Easter. A five-day festival billed as an 'exploration of the alternatives', it was a constant draw for the youth of South Australia to party, learn about new music and new fashion, and generally have a good time. Naturalism, Aboriginal lifestyles, vegetarianism, Judaism, and more were represented at each year's festival, inviting open-minded people to expand their horizons. In 1989, the festival had been shuffled around slightly and had become a celebration of the new year coming in, so there were a great many young hitchhikers out on the roads in late December.

However, after years of being preyed upon by people like Ivan Milat, and a well-publicised string of missing person cases where the vanished had last been seen hitchhiking, there was a higher degree of caution being taken now than there had been in previous years. Hitchhikers in possession of any instinct of self-preservation travelled in pairs to ensure their safety. It made a great deal of sense—one person might seem easy prey, but a pair had the advantage of numbers. Even hardened criminals would not have attempted to take on two hitchhikers alone without an accomplice in the car.

Deborah Everist and James Gibson were nineteen-year-olds in love. Both were from the Victorian suburb of Frankston, and both were headed to ConFest to celebrate the coming of a new decade that they fully intended to spend together. They were the average Australian kids, excited about the long weekend they were about to spend partying. They didn't have much money to last them the whole time they were going to be out by Albury, so they decided that the easiest way to cut corners was to hitchhike there and back. They were together, so nobody would mess with them, and on the way back from the ConFest there was sure to be dozens of new friends heading their way that they could hitch a ride with.

What they found on the road was not a friend.

Ivan picked them up on the southbound road with all of his usual manufactured charm, chatting away with the couple as they travelled, heading off the beaten track into the woodland and slowly turning the vehicle around until they were heading in a completely different direction. Up into the Belanglo State Forest where he had taken the duo of girls that he had raped before his flight to New Zealand.

Despite all his practice and all of his well-honed skills, it likely would have been extremely difficult for Ivan to successfully overpower both of the nineteen-year-olds at once. They were young, they were healthy, and they were strong. If he went toe-to-toe with the pair of them there was every likelihood that he might lose. He had his weapons stowed away in the silver four-by-four that he was driving at that point in his life—secreted away where he could get to them quickly and his unfortunate passengers could not—but even brandishing a gun wasn't always enough to get frightened prey under control. He needed more leverage than that.

The passengers grew more and more uneasy the further they travelled along the fire roads into the State Forest. While they might have believed that they were taking some shortcut originally, the increasingly rough dirt road and the absence of any hint that they were headed south began to take its toll. James, seated up front, began to make a fuss, cussing and yelling when the man wouldn't stop the car. Demanding that he take them back to the main road. Ivan didn't even seem to hear him, no matter how loud he shouted. His eyes were unfocused. It was like he was in a world of his own.

It was only when James finally bellowed at him to stop the damn car that he did as was requested. He slammed on the brakes, and James was flung forward into the dashboard. At the same moment, Ivan pulled a hunting knife from its sheath on his belt and held it out in the space that James had previously been occupying, positioned at exactly the right angle and height. As though he'd done this a dozen times or more.

He held that knife, right there, waiting for the rebound to throw James backwards into his seat again. The tip of the blade pierced through his skin, slipped between his vertebrae and bit into the boy's spinal cord. Ivan whipped the knife away again before it could do any more damage, but just that one jab had served its purpose well. James was paralyzed from the waist down. His whole body was suddenly outside of his control as he lost his torsional strength and flopped forward onto the dashboard once more.

Ivan's social circles were composed of two overlapping groups. His family, and the people that he met at gun fairs. From his family, he might have learned how to use a knife, but this particular trick was handed down to him by one of the innumerable Vietnam War veterans that were now touring Australia, making use of their expertise in weaponry to pay their way. Ivan had not spent a long time with most of them, absorbing the worst of their war stories and then moving along, but some were real fonts of horror, and those he'd taken out drinking so he could plumb the depths of their depravity. The ones who had looked into the deepest darkness of human evil and decided that they wanted more. Men who'd lived through the nightmares of Vietnam and decided that they wanted a second go around, signing up anywhere that would have them as mercenaries. To Ivan, these were his kinfolk. Men who knew violence and sex were one and the same, who knew that the whole world operated on a paper-thin lie of civilisation with reality roiling and ready underneath. Ready to explode out the moment that anyone got pushed too far.

He had learned all the tricks of the trade that war criminals had to offer, and he had brought war here.

At about the same time James was incapacitated by a well-placed blade, Deborah began screaming relentlessly, and only barely managed to get herself under control when a rifle was brandished in addition to the hunting knife. They drove a bit further down the road, James earning a cruel jab with the knife each time he made so much as a whimper.

Ivan kept on looking in the rear-view mirror, catching Deborah's eyes, like he was trying to tell her something. Like there was some reason behind all this beyond blind malice. She couldn't look away, even though she wanted to. She was so afraid. Afraid that the slightest wrong move would earn her the same treatment as her boyfriend. Afraid because they were out in the middle of nowhere, and even if she did somehow escape, there was no hope of ever finding her way home. Afraid of what would happen to James if she did make a break for it. He was completely powerless. Helpless. If she wasn't there, what would happen to him?

This maniac 'Bill' who'd picked them up could have just tossed him out of the car and it would have been a death sentence given James' current condition. He could have committed even worse torture than he was already inflicting. There was a whole world of awful terrors that Deborah had never even had to consider before in her life, dark new vistas opening up before her. She realised in those moments, trundling along the hidden roads deep in the forest that she had never really known pain or fear before, they were entirely new experiences for her.

Eventually, the car came to a halt, and she dithered there in the back seat, trying to decide whether she should abandon James and run in the desperate hope that there might be somebody in the world who would help her, or whether it was better to stay and do nothing that might antagonise Bill.

Before she'd managed to choose, Bill was out of the car, around her side and hauling her out by the hair. She was so afraid she couldn't get her body to obey her. She couldn't get her feet under her. He half-dragged and half-carried her out into the little clearing where they'd parked, then he went into the back of the car while she lay in the dry dirt hyperventilating and came back with rope.

He didn't talk to her, didn't treat her like she was a human being at all. Just set to work binding her. Trussing her up like a pig for the slaughter. The knife, still stained with James' blood, was in his hand, slicing through rope, brushing across her clothes. She could feel the sharpness of it even through the layers she wore. As though it were already pressed into her skin.

From there, Bill dragged her around by her bindings instead, hauling her through the detritus of the forest floor, deeper and deeper into the woods. He came back not long after with James slung over his shoulder, propping her poor boyfriend up against a tree so that he could see everything that was going to happen. Poor James had finally gotten his wits about him enough to speak again, but all that came out of him was a litany of false comfort and impotent drivel. He was going to get them out of here. He was going to protect her. He was going to keep her safe. She didn't have to worry. She didn't have to be scared, nothing bad was going to happen. When Bill came into sight, he'd call out to him, asking him what he wanted. Trying to buy him off. Trying to make him pay attention to him, to focus on him. It was only later that Deborah would realise that was why he was making all the noise. To try to keep Bill's attention away from her. But in the moment, she couldn't understand it at all.

The knife and the gun were left lying on a downed log when Bill wandered off again. Neither one of them could get to the weapons. Even wriggling around in the dirt like a worm couldn't get Deborah any traction. The means for them to survive and escape were right there, but she could not get to it. James was even worse off, he wasn't even bound, but the slice into his spine had left him trapped in his own body, all he could do was strain his head around, flail his arms around moving, but not getting anywhere, trying to catch a glimpse of their abductor.

He shouldn't have bothered. When Ivan wanted to be seen, he made himself seen. Still using her bindings as grips, Ivan hauled Deborah through the dirt once more until she was positioned perfectly in front of her boyfriend. Like he was putting on a show. It was only then that he went and fetched his knife from the log and set to work. His many years of hunting had forged Ivan into a proficient skinner, and cutting the clothes off a girl required barely any effort at all compared to some of the tough hides he'd parted. The areas where the rope bound cloth closely to flesh were much like the points where the skin was tightly adherent against the joints, requiring him to stretch and pull to navigate around them, slipping his blade beneath the skin and twisting his wrist to sever the connective tissue.

She was left bare as the day she was born, garbed only in the ropes and those strings of fabric still trapped beneath them. Not a single scratch on her skin could be attributed to Ivan's knife. She was untouched but for the few scratches, she sustained from being hauled around.

Untouched, until that moment.

The first rape of the day was prolonged and brutal. There was no sense of urgency, no desperate desire driving Ivan's movements. Deborah screamed and cried and tried to fight her way free, but she was completely immobilised. Even if she screamed at the top of her lungs, there was nobody for a hundred miles who might hear her. Even if she cried, there was no kind-hearted saviour who might come to her rescue. Ivan spent more time grinning over at James than he did looking at Deborah, making commentary on how lucky he was to have a girl like this, describing the specific assets that he was the most envious of as he ran his hands over them.

When tears blinded James, Ivan stopped what he was doing to clean the boy up and make sure he could see clearly before returning to the now-silent Deborah. She had already screamed herself hoarse, and whatever pain she was experiencing as he brutalised her was numbed by shock. She was retreating from the awful reality that she had found herself in, retreating into the sanctum of her own head.

Ivan wouldn't let her slip away so easily. When his rough strokes were insufficient to draw a yelp of pain anymore, he turned to open-handed slaps, pinching, and the pulling of hair to illicit the vocalizations of sheer agony that he was looking for. When even those ceased to work, he began to beat Deborah more thoroughly. The screeches of pain that his heavy punches forced out of her seemed to be exactly what he'd been craving all along, and within a few moments, he was finally done.

Or at least, that was what both of the sobbing victims hoped.

They hoped, that when he had slaked his lust, this monster might set them free, or at least kill them, so they didn't have to endure more torture, but it seemed that neither one of them would be so lucky that day.

Deborah was propped up beside James, and the two of them were left to sit there, soaked in sweat, blood and worse, as Ivan got himself a drink from the cooler and settled down to relax and recuperate. His two captives remained utterly silent so that they would not draw his attention or ire, and that suited Ivan just fine. It was hard to relax with all the yammering. He'd always preferred the quiet.

As the beers were drunk down, Ivan lined up the cans on a distant log for some target practice and then drew out the same .22 calibre rifle he'd been using to threaten James and Deborah. At almost any distance that could be achieved in the forest, he was able to hit each can dead square in the centre. It might have been a demonstration of his skill so that they knew escape was impossible, or he might simply have been feeling an absence in his daily life of anyone to whom he could show off all his terrifying talents. Who could he talk to about any of this without immediately being shipped off to jail? Who could he showcase his incredible talents to, if not his victims?

When he tired of showing off, he took up his knife once more and started to torture James. Deborah lay beside him, glassy-eyed, as Ivan pushed his hunting knife, ever so slowly, into his stomach, his legs, between his ribs. Slow careful pushes instead of violent stabs, so that James could feel the chill of the blade slipping inside him, pressing against him on the inside, slicing through skin and muscle, nicking organs, and burning all the way. He may have been paralyzed below the waist, but his senses were not impaired except for the relatively minor blood loss.

He did his best to keep quiet, to avoid doing anything to make things worse or to disturb Deborah from the safe catatonic state she had withdrawn to. It was better this way. Better that she did not see him like this. Being poked and prodded like an undercooked steak. He thought that their captor seemed pleased about his silence too. He went on thinking that until Ivan twisted the knife.

The scream, when it did come, was something truly awful, an animal sound that James didn't even know that he was capable of making. Even if someone was wandering the depths of the forest, they would hear that sound and think that it was some beast, not a man being tortured.

The shock of that abrupt noise stirred Deborah from her slumber and set her sobbing and crying all over again. She saw him as her eyes swam back into focus. Saw the blood all over him, the knife in Ivan's hand.

She started screaming too, as soon as she understood what she was seeing, the knife in Ivan's hand, in James's guts.

The smile on Ivan's face grew wider as she shrieked, but despite James' fears of what would happen if Ivan's attention was drawn back to her, he seemed quite content to let her watch as he went on stabbing his knife into James over and over until finally, the man expired.

The killing seemed to put Ivan back in the mood at last. Still drenched in her boyfriend's blood, he climbed back on top of Deborah to rape her again. All of the vigour that had been missing from their first coupling was there now; excitement seemed to have finally found him. She writhed and screamed and did everything that she could to resist him, but when she managed to hurt him by biting at his arm where he had it braced by her head, things took a more violent turn. He began to hit her, even as he went on raping her. Punching her in the face and head over and over again. She slipped in and out of consciousness, with one blow knocking her out and the next forcing her awake again. The bones in her face cracked under the flurry of blows. Her skull pounded back into the tree roots, fractured along the seams where it had sealed solid when she was just a baby.

It went on and on until he was finished, and she was dead.

After that, it was just a matter of cleaning up. Retrieving his rope from the girl's body, he wrapped it up and stowed it away, carting the cooler back to the car. He didn't worry about the beer cans. Anybody could have been drinking those out here, they wouldn't make any connection to him. Last, he laid out the bodies, James now curled up in the foetal position, Deborah still spreadeagled after the removal of her bindings, and he stacked sticks over the top of them so that they weren't in plain sight of anybody walking by. Satisfied with the day's work, he headed back to his car and went home.

Except, there were so many things wrong with that story it is difficult to count them all. From the impossibility of Ivan subduing both of the young people without a superhuman ability to do violence and intimidate, to the fact that Ivan never drank alcohol. There were dozens of individual elements throughout this version of events that did not add up. Elements that could only be explained by the presence of another person in the car with the hitchhikers. Someone that Ivan could implicitly trust, and that he would protect from prosecution by spinning this tale of his magnificence.

Two perpetrators could have kept a victim in the front and back seat of the car under control simultaneously. They could have bound both of them individually, keeping James immobile long enough for Ivan to make the surgical incision required to paralyse the man from the waist down without killing him. Two perpetrators could have transported the bound bodies of the victims around more easily. With someone else there, there would have been somebody available to drink all the beer that Ivan wouldn't touch while also still leaving someone sober enough to drive them home afterwards. Two perpetrators could have played at shooting cans together, just like they had when they were kids.

If Ivan acted alone, he would have had to do everything perfectly. Inhumanly perfectly. If he had an accomplice, he would have had a margin for error and would have planned for this crime with the same diligence that had characterised all of his previous ones. More importantly, Ivan never did anything alone. He thrived in the pack structure of his family, not as a solitary predator. Sex and violence might have been considered taboo in a normal family, things to be done behind closed doors or not at all, but the Milats did not suffer from such inhibitions. Within the bonds of their family, anything was acceptable, and they would all do their best to protect one another from the consequences if their actions were ever witnessed by an outsider. The loyalty of the Milats was like that of a secret society. A type of mutually assured destruction that prevented any one person from speaking out, as their crimes could then be revealed. There is even the possibility that the members of the family who were not naturally inclined towards criminal behaviour would have been forced to partake in such activities to provide their siblings with the necessary blackmail material to ensure their silence and loyalty.

Some days after the murders, Ivan drove further up into the forest, far from where the couple had been murdered, and he dumped their belongings out of the car window, tossing them out as he drove along one of the fire roads into the woods. Scattering them.

A hiker would later find James's camera by the roadside and take it home, not realising what it was that he'd carried off with him until weeks later when James's backpack was discovered in the same area of the park and a news report caught the hiker's attention, leading to him turning in his salvage as evidence. There were no pictures on the camera that might prove useful to the investigation, but it did at least lead the people searching for the missing teens to believe that they had disappeared in the Belanglo State Forest, working off the assumption that at some point the duo had abandoned their attempts at hitchhiking to ConFest and instead travelled out into the wilderness to do some camping for themselves, resulting in them getting lost and likely dying of exposure, or due to a lack of supplies. It was a theory that none of the victims' close family ever accepted, and it would not take long before their disbelief was vindicated.

Never Alone

After several months of living in solitude in the home that he bought for his family, Ivan became uncomfortable. He was not accustomed to being alone. Even his long car rides trawling up and down the motorways for hitchhikers and excitement were usually spent in the company of one or another of his brothers and sisters. In particular, in the aftermath of his collapsed marriage, Ivan found himself increasingly spending time with his brother Richard and his eldest sister Shirley Soire, neé Milat. Richard had always been the first to reach out to his brother in times of crisis and offer support, pulling him back into the fold in the aftermath of their father's death and helping him find work when he was struggling. Presumably, this was why, among the many affairs that Ivan carried out during this time period with his brothers' wives, Richard never suffered the same cuckolding. Yet despite this closeness, and the efforts that the man had put in through the years to stay on the best of terms, it was Shirley that Ivan seemed to be more drawn towards. She too had suffered the breakdown of a marriage, and when it happened that she found herself homeless as a result of the sale of her marital home out from under her, he offered up the spare bedroom in his house that used to belong to Jason as a place for her to stay, asking for nothing in return, not even a portion of the mortgage's monthly payments.

Instead, all that he asked of her was her company, and even that he barely asked for at all, announcing his intended plans and leaving it open as to whether Shirley wanted to come along or not. Some nights she would, and they would wend their way through the back roads and motorways by night. Other times, she would stay home or go out with her friends. Even though Ivan didn't receive her undivided attention, he still seemed to flourish as a result of the time spent with her. Not growing happier or healthier, but certainly regaining whatever confidence he had lost when his marriage collapsed.

It was with that restored confidence that he encountered a young hitchhiker by the name of Paul Onions, a visitor from the UK who was holidaying in Australia, backpacking around, staying in hostels and on the lookout for work. When Ivan switched from his routine charm offensive to the more abrasive and real personality, instead of crumbling and giving him whatever he wanted, Onions surprised his attacker, and himself, by leaping from the car and running for his life. Ivan fired shots after him, but the young Brit was able to flag down another passing car and get inside before any of the wild shots in his direction made contact. He lost all of his belongings, along with his wallet and passport, but given that he'd made it away with his life he considered himself quite lucky.

Meanwhile, Ivan didn't think twice about the bungled robbery. He didn't think that there was any way some stranger from the other side of the world was going to be able to identify him, so why bother worrying about it? It wasn't as though the world wasn't still full of stupid kids with heavy wallets that he could lighten in exchange for a ride and a scare. Hitchhikers were like a national resource—anyone was free to go and pluck them up, but most city folk didn't know what to do with them afterwards. Ivan knew exactly what he wanted to do with them. He knew how to wring every drop of value out of them: money, sex, violence, and all the other pleasures of life.

On the twentieth of January 1991, a little over a year since he took his first victims, Ivan struck again.

Simone Schmidl was a twenty-one-year-old German backpacker who had been enjoying the sights and sounds of Sydney but was now looking forward to a little remembrance from home. Her mother was flying out to meet her and join her for a camping holiday. Unfortunately, it seemed that her mother did not quite grasp the scale of Australia compared to her homeland. Instead of flying to Sydney, she had instead booked her flight to Melbourne, 600 miles to the south and an almost nine-hour journey by car, assuming that either she or Simone could lay their hands on one.

Having learned this at short notice, and with no way of contacting her mother now and asking her to change her plans, Simone had to travel across country as quickly as possible or her mother would be left standing in an airport with nobody to collect her, no means of contacting her daughter, and no idea of where she was.

To this end, Simone rose early on the morning of the twentieth, took a train from central Sydney where she stayed to one of the northern suburbs, and began hiking out along the motorway with her thumb stuck out, hoping that some kind soul might be making the massive journey to Melbourne and willing to help out a fellow traveller in need. Even if they would not be able to take her the whole way, every mile that she got closer to Melbourne would be an hour less she'd have to hitchhike with someone else. Anyone heading north or east would do; she just needed to get moving.

So, imagine her delight and surprise when a silver four-wheel-drive car pulled up at the side of the road and a local man met her with a grin, asking where she was headed. To get out of the summer sun, she climbed into the passenger seat beside him and began telling her whole tale, which he smiled and nodded his way through before announcing that he'd take her to Melbourne. She was so pleased she could have kissed him, though, of course, she did not.

The conversation was a little bit stilted. Her English was imperfect, and he was so rich in colloquialisms and localisation that it would have been near impenetrable even to a native speaker. She thought that they were talking about what a nice day it was, how long it would take to traverse the empty land between the great cities of the south, and his plans for Melbourne, yet whenever they spoke, his face seemed to be responding to an entirely different conversation. At first, she had thought that there was something off in her tone that was upsetting him, or that she was misunderstanding him entirely. Sarcasm did not always cross language barriers, so there might have been some accidental deception going on. But the harder she tried to parse out her mistake, the more confused she became.

Changing tack, she told him a little about her hometown of Regensburg, about her mother and her travels. He seemed to take it in with the same outward interest and the same sneer behind his placid expression. Simone was uncomfortable, to say the least. She knew that there was something more than a culture barrier at work here, but she had to balance that against the odds of finding anyone else willing to give her a six-hundred-mile ride for nothing.

She lapsed into a quiet state, letting her driver lead the conversation, diverting from the socially acceptable waters she'd been paddling into subjects it was never advisable to discuss with strangers. His loathing of all the immigrants coming to Australia and taking jobs that belonged to real Australian's by right. His loathing of the soft men in the cities who allowed such things to happen and hurt the real men out in the world doing real work like farming and building. All those immigrants coming in, undercutting them, stealing work from out of their hands, money from out of their pockets, food from out of their children's mouths.

By this point, Ivan was in direct competition with the latest waves of immigrants from around the world for all of the lowest-paying and hardest work in Australia. Illegal immigrants were a common sight on the worksites, and what they lacked in skill they more than made up for in willingness to work for half the going rate. His interest in politics had always been minimal, as he felt that what happened in the parliament house did not affect him, but now that he was getting paid in cash under the table just like the illegal immigrants, he could only command a wage equal to theirs. He blamed them for his change in circumstances rather than acknowledging that the situation had been created by his choice to refuse to work in any way that might provide his ex-wife with any succour.

The road rolled by and the hours rolled on, with the two of them lapsing into silence and Simone endeavouring to stare out of the window as much as possible so she wouldn't give away her distaste for the hateful man in the driver's seat. They moved off the main road and onto the tracks leading off into the forest, but the tourist did not know enough about the geography of Australia for this to raise any alarm. Since she'd arrived, she had rarely left the city at all.

She didn't even know that she was in trouble until the four-by-four came to a halt in the middle of nowhere.

Much like the last of his victims, he took her into the woods and toyed with her for hours on end. Raping her, stabbing her multiple times, and eventually leaving her body under a heap of sticks to protect it somewhat from the local wildlife. He did not even bother to pull her clothes back down from where they were rucked up around her neck before abandoning her, and by the time her body was finally discovered it would be reduced to bones, requiring dental records to be sent over from Germany to identify her.

The cause of death was only identified because of the tell-tale marks that the blade had left against the bones. In particular, an incision between two of the vertebrae used to paralyze her from the waist down and leave her helpless against Ivan's torture.

Her parents found out that she had died in possibly the cruellest way possible. A missing person's report had been filed when her mother arrived to find no sign of her daughter, and initial investigations had revealed her hitchhiking plans, but beyond that, as far as the Schmidl family knew, she was merely missing. Maybe she had failed to make it to the airport in time to meet her mother without any reliable means of transportation, maybe she had simply given up when that became apparent and settled down in one of the many small towns along the route. They had no way of proving what had happened to her until the skeleton was found wearing clothes like those she'd been reported to have been wearing at the time of her disappearance and the dental records were transferred. With the body identified, it was shipped back to Germany to be buried, The German police took custody of it and laid her to rest.

What the German police did not do was officially recognise that they had the body of Simone Schmidl. Their investigation into her status as a missing person would not be closed for several weeks, and accordingly, they made no attempt to contact her family to confirm what had been discovered. Her mother and father learned that their daughter's body had been found by hearing it on the radio news, and all of their attempts to contact the police about the 'ongoing' investigation were rebuffed.

It was only after their daughter was already in the ground and the police finally had all their paperwork in order including a duplicate copy of the Australian autopsy report that they finally made contact with the family to let them know that their daughter was dead.

By this point, the press in Germany had already moved on to new subjects, and the horrific treatment of the Schmidls by the bureaucracy was overlooked because a pair of pink jeans had been found at the same location as her corpse: Clothing that had been worn by another German tourist who had gone missing shortly after Simone.

As for whether Ivan had worked alone to abduct this young woman—who had already been primed with stories of serial killers seeking out lone women hitchhiking—it seems unlikely she would have gotten into his car without some assurance that she was safe. For example, if there was already another woman in the car. A woman like Ivan's sister Shirley, who by this point lived with him and travelled with him frequently when he went driving.

Or if she was forced into the vehicle by a pair of men, like Ivan and his brother Richard, who had been making many off-colour remarks at his place of work in a building supplies factory regarding bodies in the Belanglo, up to and including mentioning that the police still hadn't found 'the Germans' during a period when missing German tourists had not been discovered or even connected to the case yet. Though all of that pales in comparison to another conversation about the killings that he had with a co-worker, in which he said that 'stabbing a woman is like cutting a loaf of bread' and boasted, 'There's more out there they haven't found yet.'

It was entirely possible that he simply had knowledge of the crimes second hand, from talking to his siblings, but the specific detail of the sensation that you experience when pushing a knife into someone's body seemed to suggest that he was more involved than that.

Between the death of that first German hitchhiker and the next pair, almost a whole year passed by, supposedly without Ivan committing any acts of brutality. There were a great many missing people during this time, particularly missing hitchhikers, but no bodies were discovered, and no connection was made. By this time, not even the bodies of his first victims had been spotted. He was killing people for fun and not only getting away with it but getting away with it to the degree that nobody had even realised there were any bodies in the woods yet.

The young couple of Gabor Neugebauer and Anja Habschied were staying at the King's Cross Backpacker's Inn in Sydney over Christmas, but on Boxing Day of 1991, it was time for them to head out. They were heading to Darwin, eventually, with plans to stop off in Adelaide along the way. They were young and headstrong, with no fear of the boogeymen that other hitchhikers spoke about. They were together, so they knew that they would be alright.

Gabor was the first victim to be found dead by gunshot instead of stabbing. He had been trussed up and then used for target practice. Dozens of bullet wounds had perforated his body before he was eventually untied, laid out and covered in brush. Meanwhile, his girlfriend had suffered a more gruesome fate than any of the previous victims. Her body was discovered missing the tell-tale pair of pink jeans that she had last been seen wearing when she departed Sydney, along with her underwear, suggesting that she had been raped like all the other women, but it was above the waist, and indeed at the shoulders, that her corpse took a turn for the more brutal. She had been decapitated; her head sawn from her neck with a large hunting knife.

Examination of the scene would later reveal that in addition to the many shots that had struck home in Gabor's body, over a hundred casings from the .22 bullets fired from Ivan's uncommon Ruger rifle were discovered scattered about the scene. Before he had made the shots that had killed the twenty-year-old, he had toyed with him, shooting all around him, without ever hitting him. Making a show of his exceptional marksmanship, before making mocking 'mistakes' as Gabor's girlfriend was forced to watch in horror.

Gabor had been gagged, and at some point, strangled, suggesting that he had struggled and made more noise than the previous victims, to the degree that it irritated Ivan and any accomplices to a point that they felt the need to intervene and make him stop.

There was also evidence found on the body that the victims had been bound, set loose, and then bound again. Moved from one location to the next without the need for dragging them around. Proceeding deeper into the woods so that they'd be out of sight and earshot of even the fire roads that only the locals might know and use.

Ivan wasn't just killing freely—he was beginning to experiment with his methods, seeking out the most pleasurable order of events and combinations of torments. There was no evidence that Gabor had been paralyzed during his torture, but an examination of Anja's body suggested that she had. Instead of rendering the larger threat incapable, Ivan now left the man in the relationship capable of movement while he raped the woman, letting his male victim watch and struggle to fight free of his bondage. Every choice he made was born of pure sadism, each experiment carefully designed to explore new ways to maximize the suffering and cruelty of the killing. With Gabor already injured and bleeding to death, the decapitation of Anja would have served as a particularly gratifying and messy climax to events.

Of the two victims, Ivan was incapable of empathising in any way with the woman, instead interpreting events solely through the eyes of the man over whom he was asserting his dominance. The power of empathy was inverted by his sadism, with Ivan using his understanding of the other man's emotional state as a roadmap to guide him to utter psychological devastation. At least he believed in the humanity of the men. If they were devoid of humanity, there would be no pleasure to be taken in stripping it away. The women, however, were merely tools to be used to that end.

Given his choice to commit adultery with his brother's wife, and the rumours of the affairs that he carried out with his other brother's wives, it seems likely that there was an element of cruelty in cuckolding that he found particularly pleasing. His entire early life had been structured like a social-Darwinist nightmare, with the strong ruling over the weak, and whoever asserted dominance getting the lion's share of the sustenance— whether that was food in a literal sense or the attention and affections of the family.

For Ivan, sex was just another prize to be won, a pleasure to be taken when he had earned it, through superiority or trickery. But he wasn't completely detached from reality. He understood the emotional attachments that sex formed and had even experienced what he had thought of as love at one time. And like everything else that Ivan had learned about in his life, he used that new knowledge like a bludgeon to deal harm to everyone around him. If he had studied dentistry, then his victims would likely have been found with holes drilled in their teeth. Whatever he knew, he used.

Sex and violence were what he knew. Emotional manipulation and abuse. Gunplay, hunting, cutting and gutting. The terrain of the Belanglo. Everything that had ever entered his mind became a tool to be used against everyone else in the world, initially out of some survival instinct driving him to dominate, but now simply for the joy of seeing others hurt as badly as he could hurt them.

And just as they always had been, it seems that his submissive siblings were following his lead, though, of course, none of them would ever speak out of turn and let that slip. It was against their family's signature code of silence.

Run Riot

On April 18, 1992, Joanne Walters and Caroline Clark, two British tourists barely out of their teenage years, left King's Cross to hitchhike together, to pick up some seasonal work picking fruit to finance the rest of their trip. They had heard that there was work available in Victoria, so they headed out in that direction almost as soon as they'd arrived in Sydney. At Bulli Pass, near Wollongong, they were spotted alive one final time, asking locals for directions to the Hume Highway, where Ivan had picked up all of his victims to date.

As with the previous pairs, they were taken, bound, raped, and tortured before finally being murdered and hidden under brush. Clarke had been the subject of Ivan's target practice this time around, with her body showing ten separate bullet wounds, while Walters had been on the receiving end of the more personal attention that he doled out with the knife, paralyzed, and then stabbed repeatedly in non-lethal locations until she eventually expired from blood loss. The same pattern, endlessly repeating. Hitchhikers convinced that they would remain safe in their travels, despite ever-increasing media warnings against such practices, believing that travelling in pairs would somehow safeguard them from the likes of monsters such as Ivan.

Walters and Clark marked the final victims that would officially be tied to Ivan Milat. However, to those familiar with criminology, there was little logic to this. Once Ivan had begun killing, there was no reason for him to limit himself to only one or two victims a year. Furthermore, the confidence with which he performed fairly complex acts of abduction and torture strongly suggests that he had markedly more experience committing these types of crimes than the official accounting of the dead can explain. In terms of pure statistics, for a serial killer to begin murdering at the age of forty-five is extremely unlikely, with most late bloomers beginning their campaigns of terror in their thirties at the latest.

The fact that Ivan was so incredibly mobile across huge areas of Australia throughout most of his working life when he was almost always travelling entirely alone with no other source of entertainment, would suggest that the limited geographical area in which all his confirmed killings had taken place was probably only a small fraction of the hunting ground that he'd have had access to in his earlier years.

In the years that followed the investigation into what became dubbed the 'Backpacker Murders', many more bodies would be found in the areas where Ivan was already known to dump them. Bodies that could be attributed to no other serial killer, and which would all fit neatly into the timeline of Ivan's degeneration from a family man to a sadistic killer.

On February 26, 1971, Keren Rowland disappeared. She was due to meet her sister at a motel in Canberra and never showed up, though they both departed from the same place at the same time. Her abandoned car was later discovered in an undeveloped area, and later that year, her bones would be discovered fifteen feet off the footpath to the Fairburn Pine Plantation Air Disaster Memorial. She was pregnant at the time of her death. It was not considered murder until many years later when the scene of her discovery was compared with the scenes discovered in Belanglo.

On November 13, 1987, Peter Letcher tried to hitchhike to his parent's house in Bathurst. Early the next year, his bones were discovered by hikers on a woodland track close to the Jenolan Caves, a site that Ivan had taken his then-wife Karen to visit shortly before she escaped from their abusive marriage. The murder had taken place shortly after she had finally left Ivan. Peter was found face down, covered in branches like all of Ivan's other victims. He had been handcuffed, shot in the head with a .22 calibre gun like the one that Ivan used in his other crimes, and stabbed in the back repeatedly.

There was also some question over whether or not the man had been sexually assaulted, but there was no way to confirm it due to the level of decay that had occurred in the extreme summer heat.

On September 6, 1991, another woman would go missing while hitchhiking. Dianne Pennacchio had been staying at the Lake George Hotel in Bungedore but was heading home to Queanbeyan now that her stay was done, informing a friend that she meant to catch a ride on the same stretch of the King's Highway that Paul Onions and Ivan's other victims were abducted from.

Two months later. her body was discovered by Forestry Commission workers in Tallaganda State Forest, covered in branches, nude from the waist up though showing all signs from her dishevelled clothing that she too had been a victim of sexual assault. Most tellingly, there was a single incision into her spine that had rendered her paralyzed and helpless to flee. A stab into the seventh thoracic vertebrae that had become Ivan's calling card. Her death occurred in the middle of the cluster of murders for which Ivan was eventually convicted, filling in one of the gaps when he seemed to be inexplicably inactive.

An entirely different serial killer was believed to be at work in the Hunter Region south of Newcastle, but on further investigation following Ivan's identity becoming public, many witnesses placed him at the scenes of the crimes. In addition, they took place during a time when his work for the roads commission would have had him operating in that area.

Leanne Goodall was last seen at Newcastle's Star Hotel on December 30, 1978. Ivan was known to frequent the hotel in those days, and it is known that Leanne had every intention of departing for Sydney on the day she was last seen and could easily have been tempted by the offer of a free ride.

Robyn Hickie vanished four months later from a bus stop opposite her home in Belmont North. The police initially believed that she was just another eighteen-year-old runaway, but Milat was staying at the Belmont Hotel on the night before she vanished, so it is feasible she represented an opportunity too tempting to ignore.

Amanda Robinson was only fourteen when she went missing on April 29, a few weeks later. She was last seen walking along Lake Road in Gateshead following a school dance. This kicked off a thorough police investigation that would ultimately prove to be fruitless.

Amanda Zolis was last seen on October 12 of the same year, heading off to the Christian Café in Newcastle. She spoke to her father on the phone, explaining that she meant to buy clothes for her upcoming trip to Queensland, before vanishing without a trace shortly after the call was made. She was sixteen years old.

Annette Briffa had been alternating between staying in Asquith in northern Sydney and on the Central Coast. She was last seen by witnesses hitchhiking in the direction of Hornsby on the tenth of January 1980. She was picked up by an orange Mazda, the same colour and make of car that Ivan was driving at the time.

Finally, there was Susan Isenhood, who disappeared while hitchhiking to Taree. Her remains would not be discovered until 1986, in Possum Brush in the Kiwarrak State Forest, by which time advanced decomposition precluded any possibility of a detailed analysis of her final hours.

Beyond these cases where there was an extremely obvious connection to Ivan Milat, either in terms of methodology or opportunity, there were a further twenty-three cases where he was considered a likely culprit. In most of these cases, there was such a complete lack of any physical evidence that there was no point in proceeding with prosecution as it would be entirely insufficient to secure a conviction. Even in those cases where there was some sort of obvious link, it was deemed insufficient to progress any further investigation.

Anita Cunningham and Robyn Hoinville-Bartam were student nurses and roommates hitchhiking to Queensland. Anita's body was never found. Robyn was found half-naked beneath a bridge, raped, and shot in the head with the same .22 calibre rifle that Ivan liked best.

Gabrielle Jahnke and Michelle Riley were hitchhiking from Brisbane to the Gold Coast. Gabrielle's body was found at the bottom of a steep slope off the Pacific Highway, but Michelle was eventually discovered in isolated bushland with her underwear missing and her dress pushed up. Branches had been placed over her body, matching Ivan's usual body disposal methodology.

Lydia Notz was last seen on October 31, 1976, at a friend's apartment. She left a note saying that she would be back in a week and then vanished off the face of the earth.

Narelle Mary Cox is one of the few victims for whom Ivan had some sort of alibi to defend him. When she went missing from the Brunswick Heads area of New South Wales, Ivan had been signed into work. The police, when contacted by her family, took this to mean that he could not have been responsible for her disappearance. Unfortunately, Ivan's workmates were all in the habit of clocking one another in to avoid anyone getting into trouble, so it was entirely possible that he was nowhere near the work site where he was registered.

Barbara Carol Brown, a young American, vanished in May of 1978 while hitchhiking to Queensland.

Stephen Lapthorne and his girlfriend, Michelle Pope, both vanished on August 25 of the same year. His car was never found, nor were either of their bodies. In 2005, both were declared dead but no further details were offered up by the coroner.

On the eleventh of January 1979, Alan Fox and his girlfriend Anneke Adriaansen disappeared while hitchhiking away from Byron Bay, an area in which Milat was working at the time.

Toni Maree Cavanagh and Kay Docherty were heading to a disco in Wollongong on July 27 when they disappeared. The girls were 15 and 16, respectively.

Kim Cherie Teer disappeared in September while hitchhiking with her dog in East Melbourne. She had previously expressed a fear of hitchhiking following the recent spate of disappearances and was considering getting a driving license when she vanished.

Elaine Johnson and Kerry Ann Joel vanished while hitchhiking to Wyong on February 1, 1980. Milat was working in the area at the time.

In June of the same year, Deborah Balken and Gillian Jamieson, both twenty-year-old student nurses, were picked up from a tavern in Parramatta by a man who matched Ivan's description and were never seen again.

Joanne Lacey and Lesley David Toshak both vanished while hitchhiking to Byron Bay in April.

Carmen Verheyden was hitchhiking home after a party on March 10, 1991, when she went missing.

Finally, Melony and Chad Sutton went missing in November of 1992, shortly before Ivan was forcibly stopped. They had been sent off to school in Queensland but allegedly planned to hitchhike to find their father in Perth, a route that would have taken them through Belanglo State Forest. They remain missing, with no further information ever surfacing.

If Ivan Milat was responsible for even a fraction of these crimes, it would certainly help to fill in a few of the many blank pages of his story. The degree to which he escalated from non-violent crimes to full-on sadistic torture so rapidly made no sense, but these crimes, should they indeed be his, would help explain his swift devolution by making it markedly less swift. It would also help to explain why he so often bragged of the many more victims in the outback that the police had never and would never find.

Basic statistics, given the vast areas of unoccupied land that Ivan was operating in, would seem to suggest that it is extremely unlikely that investigators have turned up all the bodies for which he is responsible. Even if you do not believe that the majority of cases tied to his name were his responsibility, it is impossible to discount the idea that he was behind at least some of them.

Task Force Air

In September of 1992, two orienteering enthusiasts were exploring Belanglo when they uncovered a concealed corpse. The next day, the police would discover a second decaying body concealed much the same way, under some branches, and located just a short walk from the first. Via dental records, these were identified as the bodies of Joanna Walters and Caroline Clarke. After a thorough search of the forest around these awful discoveries, the police concluded that there was nothing else to find and departed.

In October of the next year, another pair of corpses were discovered when a local man was out collecting firewood: the bodies of Gibson and Everist. This sparked confusion in the police as his camera and backpack had both shown up at Galston Gorge, 75 miles to the north.

This time the police were not satisfied that they had found everything that was out there. They began sweeping the forest for evidence of more bodies, and on the first of November they would discover the skeleton of Simone Schmidl, accompanied by a pair of pink jeans that had not belonged to her, but to Anja Habschied. This latest breadcrumb led the police on until they discovered the bodies of Habschied and Gabor Neugebauer on a fire trail in a pair of shallow graves.

Examination of these bodies determined that they had been tortured and mutilated while still alive, and this in turn resulted in the formation of Task Force Air by the New South Wales Police, containing over twenty detectives and analysts determined to get to the bottom of these crimes. A few weeks later, the already busy team had their lives kicked into overdrive, as the local government offered up a $500,000 reward for information that led to the arrest and prosecution of whoever was responsible for these terrible crimes. In addition, a full pardon was offered to anyone who was involved in the crimes that had not taken place in the murders. Even then, the police recognised that more likely than not, Ivan had not been working alone.

They were inundated with information, more than even the prodigious workforce that they had assembled was capable of handling. Endless calls from everyone and anyone who thought that their missing friend or family member might have fallen victim to the same killer. Anyone even tangentially related to the deceased who had been discovered, trying to offer up every scrap of detail that might help justice be done.

The problem was no longer a lack of information about their killer; it was the balance of signal to noise. They were receiving so much information that it was drowning out the aspects that were relevant. Computers and data technology were employed, cutting edge for the time, and they were able to narrow their suspect list down to only 230 men. Speculation abounded both within the task force and without, as the various methods used to kill these victims suggested that they were not dealing with a single killer but multiple murderers with their own pathologies. But the investigation pressed on working from the assumption that there was only one criminal to be arrested for everything.

On the other side of the world, Paul Onions turned on his television and saw a news report about the killings, specifically about the location from where the victims were believed to have been abducted. Without even checking the time difference, he called the Australian embassy and then the tip line that Task Force Air had put together.

His report sat on a computer screen next to a phone for a day or so, ignored in the influx, but finally, the data analysis system that the team had been using picked up the keywords in his statement: the dates and the times, the vehicles described, and the methodology of the abduction.

After the team had thoroughly investigated the initial police report, in April of 1994, Paul Onions received a callback.

At his own expense, Paul took time off work and flew back to Australia to assist with the investigation, successfully identifying 'Bill' from the hundreds of suspect photographs presented to him. Combined with other reports that the Task Force had been receiving from the various people that Ivan Milat had encountered over the years, the police now had all the probable cause that they needed to arrest him and search his house for evidence of a connection to the murders.

Arresting a man like Ivan Milat presented its own host of problems, however. He was heavily armed and militant in his commitment to the ideals of self-defence against state power. Everyone who knew him talked about his obsession with firearms and the abundance of them that he surrounded himself with. If they attempted to send a couple of officers to make the arrest as they would anyone else, in all likelihood, the outcome would be two dead officers and their prime suspect on the run.

A tactical response had to be formulated, and in the end, after days of surveillance of Ivan's home on Eagle Street, during which he was often seen observing the officers through his own binoculars, the task force dispatched fifty armed officers to place him under arrest, completely encircling the home with snipers before sending armed police smashing through the door.

Milat was caught with his trousers down, quite literally, in bed with a new girlfriend. He had no chance to arm himself or fight the police off. Everything had gone as smoothly as it possibly could have. However, the vast hoard of illegal weaponry that was supposedly in the house was nowhere to be seen. There was a single hunting rifle that did not match the profile of the one used in the killings, and parts of a second rifle that ballistics experts believed was the .22 Ruger that they had been searching for. Without the barrel of the illegal weapon to compare to the rifling marks on the bullets, they could not prove it was the same gun that had been used.

Ivan had caught wind of the investigation.

Wally, along with some of Ivan's other siblings, had been interviewed as part of the police search for their killer, and they had immediately reported back to Ivan about what they had heard and seen. In turn, he had taken the arsenal that he kept stored in his home and hidden it. Even the parts of the .22 that were found had been secreted away in a hiding place that he had built into the drywall of the home instead of being out in the open. In his sister's room in the house, they found sleeping bags that they believed belonged to two of the hikers, but it would be easy enough for Ivan to claim that she had come upon those on her own and that he was not responsible for the behaviour of what was essentially a lodger. Without more, he was going to slip through the fingers of the police.

They arrested him for the abduction of Paul Onions and used that as a solid enough excuse to get him off the streets before he could do more harm, or destroy more evidence, but they needed the rest of the weaponry to make the case against Ivan stick.

Luckily, the local judiciary considered the circumstantial evidence that the Task Force had gathered as sufficient cause to issue warrants to search other properties that Ivan had access to, and after a top-to-bottom search of Wally's house and his mother's home, the remainder of the .22 rifle, along with a wide assortment of other illegal weaponry, was uncovered. Alex Milat was also re-interviewed. He had provided false testimony to the police in relation to the case months prior, presumably at the behest of his brother. He had claimed to see two four-by-four vehicles driving by with the missing women on board, along with a whole gang of murderers of various descriptions. It was enough to pique their interest, so his home was also searched and two backpacks were found that had belonged to the German girls.

Wally and Alex Milat were both brought up on firearms charges with the expectation that they would blame Ivan for the weapons being on their property, providing further evidence against him, but neither would speak out against Ivan, even now.

It did not matter. The police felt that they had enough to add the charges for the murders to Ivan's docket, even without the leverage of proof that the recovered arsenal had belonged to him. Among the other things found in Wally's house were many articles of women's clothing that he had gifted to his wife. Items that were identified as belonging to the missing hitchhikers. Enough circumstantial evidence that they believed they could lock in a conviction, given how motivated any jury would be to have Ivan locked away and the whole horrid history of these brutal murders put to rest.

Almost immediately after receiving the new list of charges, Ivan fired his family lawyer and made attempts to fundraise for a better defender. He was eventually provided with a lawyer by the state through legal aid when his attempts failed.

Over two hundred witnesses were heard by the court, providing piecemeal information about Ivan's movements, his history, his temperament, and all the other vital facts on which the state was building its case.

Meanwhile, his state-appointed lawyer did a surprisingly solid job given the tide of public opinion, and even in the run-up to the trial, when Ivan was interviewed by the press, he remained convinced that he would be found innocent. A recorded phone call from the time had Ivan saying, 'I didn't do it, I don't know who did it. It is up to them to prove my guilt, not me to prove my innocence.'

It was an entirely accurate depiction of the trial as it stood. There was no evidence against Ivan that was not entirely circumstantial in terms of the murders. Nothing to directly link him to any crime. All that the police had were the weapons and his whereabouts. Weapons that he of course claimed were available to anyone who had access to his home, or the homes of anyone in his large family.

In essence, his defence was the same one that had seen him walk away scot-free a dozen or more times as a teenager—that any one of his siblings could be responsible for the crimes that he was being accused of, and unless the court could prove exactly which one of the Milat kids had done the wicked deed itself, they could not charge him with the crime.

His lawyer leaned into this heavily, highlighting repeatedly the fact that Ivan could not have committed the murders by himself, and that it was considerably more likely that if he were involved at all, then it would be as a part of the family, not as an individual. Every one of his brothers was named as a potential killer. Even his sister who co-habited with him was named as a potential accomplice who could have provided the real killer with the weaponry that was the only thing that tied him to the case.

It was a legally sound argument, and all of the evidence that was presented to the jury throughout the trial was exactly as circumstantial as his lawyer insisted that it was; however, the jury was convinced by the sheer volume of it that he was not only responsible for the crimes but the sole person to have committed them. Task Force Air presented their profile of the killer and matched every detail of it to Ivan's life. Records from all of his employers throughout the years were wheeled out to show that he was in the right place at the right time to have committed the crimes. Ballistics experts showed the skill with which the .22 Ruger Rifle had been used throughout the abductions, and evidence showed that Ivan had learned the paralyzing knife thrust from his connections in the illegal arms trade. All of those tiny grains of sand were added to one side of the scales of justice with Ivan's claims of utmost innocence on the other, and the scales tilted.

Despite his lawyer's attempts to shift blame onto them, all of Ivan's siblings showed up in court, offering up alibis for the times when Ivan was alleged to be committing these crimes.

On July 27, 1996, after a gruelling eighteen weeks of testimony, the jury found Ivan Milat guilty of all the crimes he had been charged with, and he was sentenced to life without the possibility of parole for each one. He was additionally convicted of the attempted murder, false imprisonment, and robbery of Paul Onions, the man who had inadvertently brought him down, for which he was issued an additional eighteen years, although by this point any additional time added to his sentence was essentially moot as he would be dead long before having the chance to serve out all his sentenced time.

From that point onwards, Ivan made multiple appeals against his conviction, arguing that he had not received legal representation, on the basis that competent legal counsel would have been able to convince the jury that there was no actual evidence tying him to the crime. This was dismissed by the court of criminal appeals, resulting in Ivan applying to the High Court of Australia that he be allowed leave to appeal for a different reason. This was also dismissed, resulting in his finally taking his case to the New South Wales Supreme Court in 2005, where it was once more rejected, reaffirming that the original trial had been both fair and just.

Yet even from the beginning, it was apparent to Ivan that he was never going to receive the freedoms that he felt he was entitled to through legal means. If he meant to get out of prison, or at least receive the level of comfort to which he felt he was entitled, then he needed to get creative.

Caged Monster

On the first day that he arrived in Maitland Gaol, Ivan approached his new life with the same swagger and confidence that had carried him through all of his previous stays behind bars. He had always been the biggest and the toughest, and nobody had ever given him any trouble.

But news of the vile crimes that he had committed against innocent young women had spread before his arrival. There would be no warm welcome from old friends waiting for Ivan this time around. Instead, on the very first day in a communal area, he was beaten unconscious and left for dead.

From that point forward, Ivan was a lot less ostentatious, travelling carefully around the prison and trying to ensure that he was always in the company of other prisoners that he felt he could trust. Or failing that, keeping himself in plain view of one of the guards.

In another high-profile prisoner, he found something of a kindred spirit. George Savvas had been a city councilman who was discovered to be the kingpin of the local drug trade, and like Ivan, he had now abandoned all hope of legal recourse getting him out of prison.

Over the course of the following year, the two of them, and two other inmates, formed a conspiracy to escape from the prison, collecting the materials that they thought they would need and readying themselves for the attempt. There was a single guard stationed in the reception room that they meant to pass through, and the entire plan hinged on his being killed before he could raise any sort of alarm. This was Ivan's part of Savvas's plan. He had everything else that he needed, but in Milat, he had a skilled killer. Savvas had also given some consideration to the manhunt that would inevitably follow their escape. He reasoned that taking the infamous serial killer Ivan Milat alone would guarantee that public and law enforcement attention would focus primarily on his recapture leaving Savvas in the shadows to make a more circumspect exit from the country before anyone cared that he was even involved.

Fortunately for the guard stationed in the reception area that night, word of the plan slipped out from one of their other conspirators and made its way to the warden.

Now aware of what was unfolding, Warden Debus allowed the prisoners to proceed with their plan, escaping their cells and picking locks until they came upon a squad of heavily armoured and armed officers on loan from the police's Major Incident Group. Their escape was over before it had even begun.

The following day, facing an even longer prison sentence, Savvas committed suicide in his cell, hanging himself. Ivan had no opportunity to mourn the loss of his 'friend', however, as he was immediately sent along to the maximum-security section at Goulburn Correctional Centre, where he was to serve out the rest of his sentences, at least until 2001, when the newly constructed 'Supermax' High-Risk Management Corrections Centre was built at Goulburn and he was transferred there, instead.

Almost immediately, Ivan objected to the new circumstances he had been placed into. Deliberately eating razor blades, staples, and other metal objects in a ploy to be transferred to a mental health facility, where he felt he'd be more comfortable. After they were surgically removed, he was returned to his new cell once more.

Another escape attempt soon followed, with a saw blade hidden inside a packet of biscuits in his room that he meant to use to cut his way out of his cell at night. It was found during a routine search using a metal detector. A routine search that had, in truth, only become necessary because of his repeated attempts at self-harm.

In 2006, he came back into the limelight of public attention when it was learned that his new cell had a toaster oven and television, the same as every other cell in the new block, provided to ensure that prisoners did not have to share communal areas. There was public outcry at these comforts being offered to him and legal challenges made to their provision.

In January of 2009, after his final appeal to the high court had failed, Ivan decided to take matters into his own hands once more. Intent on scaring the Supreme Court into reconsidering their position, he decided to mail them a little something to convince them how serious he was. Using a plastic knife, he sawed through the skin, muscle, and connective tissue holding his little finger in place and managed to sever it entirely.

Shockingly, he was not able to get the finger out through the prison mail service but did land himself in Goulburn Base Hospital, where it was quickly discovered that surgery to re-attach the finger would not be possible due to the exceedingly messy job he had done in removing it. He was sent back to his cell the following day, no longer able to count past nine.

For a time, there were no more attempts at self-harm, then in 2011, Ivan learned about the Sony Playstation. He was determined to have one of them in his cell and committed himself to a hunger strike until his demands were met. He went without food for nine days, losing over 2 stone in weight before finally giving in and eating. He would never know the joy of a PlayStation console.

Once more, there was a long period of silence until May of 2019, when it was discovered that he was suffering from oesophageal cancer. He received treatment for it before being transferred to Long Bay Correctional Centre, though his sickness progressed rapidly, resulting in massive weight loss and his final transfer to the Prince of Wales Hospital.

On October 27, 2019, Ivan Milat died of oesophageal and stomach cancer at the age of 74, leaving a final request that the state be forced to pay for his funeral. The request was denied by the Corrections Minister, and money was instead extracted from Ivan's prison account to reimburse the full cost of his cremation.

In his final year, Ivan was visited repeatedly and constantly by criminologists and the police, all seeking to extract some sort of confession from him, looking for some sort of closure for the many families who believed that he had killed their children. Throughout it all, Ivan maintained his innocence, casting blame onto his siblings, most of whom had died many years before. There would be no closure for anyone. Ivan still held the pettiest amount of power over other people with the knowledge that he possessed, and to the very last moment, he would not let any of it slip away. He did not care about other people, he did not care about their feelings, all he cared about was what advantage he could extract from the situation, and there was no pay-off for telling the truth.

While there was no deathbed confession from Milat, two people close to him did let some things slip in their final moments. His mother Margaret spoke of what her son had done as she lay dying, admitting that while he had never officially confessed, he had confided in her that he was responsible for the murders. Similarly, when his barrister from the original court case, Terry Martin, was on his deathbed, he shared one salient detail that he had never been able to disclose before. Ivan had admitted that his sister Shirley accompanied him when he raped and killed the victims that he was being tried for. She had been present, laughing and drinking as he had brutalised them. This type of confession is obviously inadmissible in the court of law, and a breach of confidentiality, but it does help to explain many of the gaps in the stories being told by both the prosecution and the defence if Ivan was to be believed.

As for his other siblings, each one of them has, at various points throughout their lives, let details slip that suggested a far greater knowledge of Ivan's crimes than could be expected from innocent bystanders.

When confronted by the press, Richard Milat was asked whether he feared that he would be arrested, but he laughed it off, saying 'If they were going to get me for them, they would have got me by now.'

Boris Milat on the other hand, the young brother who had done his best to escape from his family's long shadow, had other opinions on the matter. He met with the press only under the condition of anonymity, not wanting any of his siblings to be able to track him down. He told them, 'All my brothers are capable of extreme violence, given the right time and place... The things I can tell you are much worse than what Ivan's meant to have done. Everywhere he's worked, people have disappeared. I know where he's been.'

When asked whether he believed his brother was guilty of the crimes for which he had been charged, Boris gave a troubling answer. 'If Ivan's done these murders, I reckon he's done a hell of a lot more.'

When pressed for a number he replied, 'About twenty-eight.' A match to the twenty-one additional killings that the police were unable to gather enough evidence to connect to Ivan.

Ivan Milat left an indelible mark on Australian culture, with many a recounting of his crimes throughout the years in the form of books and television shows. The film Wolf Creek was based on the mythos of the murderous outback dweller and proved popular enough to win awards and attention around the world.

Yet the Milat family did not abruptly cease existing just because of Ivan's newfound fame. The ever-expanding family tree continued to grow in the area where he had once hunted, and recently some of his nephews have faced legal troubles as a result of following in the footsteps of their most famous relative. Rape charges, and illegal ownership of weapons, these things still flare up every now and again, and the name Milat is still well known to the local police. Because ultimately, Ivan was not the only product of the household in which he was raised, only the best known. All of his brothers had the same upbringing and values instilled in them, and all of their children were raised by men who lived those lives. Some of them might have been able to escape the awful burden of heredity and indoctrination, but not all of them. Not enough of them.

From the day that he was born, Ivan Milat was made to compete with his siblings for survival. He was raised to be the strongest, the toughest, the meanest, and taught that to be anything else was akin to suicide. Only the strong survived in the world that he experienced, so he meant to make himself the strongest of the strong and to show everyone around him at every opportunity that there was no brutality or depravity that he would not pursue so long as it kept them all living in fear of him.

When everyone was afraid of him, Ivan won. The moment that they started to think for themselves, he was in danger. That was what his father had taught him. That was what every beating that he had suffered throughout his youth had reinforced. Get caught, get told on, and suffer. Bludgeon everyone around you into supporting you blindly, and you went without the pain.

There were a few different moments throughout his life when things might have gone differently, and his story might have turned out considerably less memorable and considerably more pleasant. When he had his beloved little sister to serve as a moral anchor, keeping him from going too far off the deep end for fear of losing her love and respect. When he recreated the same dynamic with his teenage bride. These were opportunities for him to look at the world in which he believed that he lived and see it for the falsehood that it was, but each time, he lacked the self-awareness or the desire for self-examination that would have been required to improve himself. Ill fortune snatched his little sister from him, hardening his heart and making him worse, and in turn, when he had the opportunity to leave behind the hard life he had forged for himself and settle into a life like anyone else's with his new wife, he sabotaged it all. He was not willing to wait for life to snatch his joy away from him, so he went about destroying it all on his own. He was, by all accounts, a good father, showing kindness to a boy that he did not sire, which many men of the time could not have countenanced, but his inability to see his wife as a person rather than a prize that he had won, with her own desires and needs, resulted in her becoming his punching bag, forced to flee for her own survival, rather than becoming his salvation.

There can be no denying that Ivan Milat was an evil man, but the question remains as to how much of that was a product of his upbringing as opposed to some wickedness that was inherent in him. He had the intelligence and drive that, in another family, might have helped him to excel in life. Given the right start, he could have been a leader in the industry, a contributor to society or even a healer, but because of how he was brought up outside of society, he instead became a monster. Excelling in the only things that he believed that he was capable of.

To examine the mind of Ivan Milat is not to consider the complex psychology of a man, but the base nature of a beast. A creature of instinct, driven to cruelty because it proved his dominance. Dominance was all that Ivan Milat cared about. It was not enough for him to be the best, it was not enough to have the respect of others—he needed their absolute submission. He had to prove to them that he was not only better and stronger than them, but that to cross him in any way would result in their humiliation and destruction.

This was the fantasy that he was acting out with his victims, not some joyful delusion that gave him sexual release like so many sadists, but the fantasy that he was all-powerful over them. That was the appeal of abducting, raping, and torturing. To establish his power over them, and by extension, over anyone who witnessed his crimes. The message that he was trying to convey, whether consciously or not, to whichever of his siblings were along for the ride was that just as easily as he had taken these strangers and robbed them of their power, he could do the same unto them. This was what the strange pseudo-incestuous affairs that he conducted with his siblings' wives were about, too, proving that he could take anything from them if he so willed it. He could outshoot them, he could outfight them, there was no limit to the things that he was willing to do to prove that he was stronger and better than them. Any one of his brothers could have been lying there in the dirt, paralysed with a single thrust of Ivan's knife. Any one of his sisters could have been tied up, with her dress shoved up and her panties discarded. This could have been any one of them, or anyone that they loved, and neither the law nor any sense of decency would stop Ivan from doing whatever the hell he pleased, whenever he pleased, so they had better toe the line and remain obedient to him because the alternative would be for them to become his enemy. They did not want to be his enemy. Look at what happened to the people that Ivan considered his enemy. Look at the piles of sticks you couldn't drive for an hour through the forest without seeing, think about the bones that might be under any one of them. Think about what it would mean to cross him. Think about whose bones would be under the next pile of sticks.

His family was his entire world, the only people whose opinions and thoughts actually mattered, not because he cared about them or loved them, but because they, too, had been raised to be apex predators in a world full of sheep, and he wanted to be sure that they knew he was the alpha.

Ivan was not a unique monster. The world is absolutely bursting with people who believe that they are better than everyone else, and who are willing to do whatever they consider necessary to prove it. Within the confines of society, this produces ambition and drive, people who are willing to push themselves beyond the limits of what was thought possible to achieve incredible things, but without the rules and confines of society, the result is something entirely different.

Psychopaths are all different, both from the regular person and from other psychopaths. Each one of them has their own unique pathology, shaped by the lives that they have lived, and the ways that different parts of their brains have connected violence with pleasure. But what could be considered the most notable thing about Ivan Milat is how very common his particular pathology is.

Every chest-thumping 'alpha male' in the world harbours fantasies of what kind of violence they might unleash if they were driven to it. Every one of them is convinced that they are the best, and willing to do whatever is required to prove it. The only difference between them and Ivan Milat is their definition of what is required.

Every Review Helps

If you enjoyed the book and have a moment to spare, I would really appreciate a short review on Amazon. Your help in spreading the word is gratefully received and reviews make a huge difference to helping new readers find me. Without reviewers, us self-published authors would have a hard time!

Type in your link below to be taken straight to my book review page.

US	geni.us/ooUS
UK	geni.us/ooUK
Australia	geni.us/ooAUS
Canada	geni.us/ooCA

Thank you! I can't wait to read your thoughts.

About Ryan Green

Ryan Green is a true crime author who lives in Herefordshire, England with his wife, three children, and two dogs. Outside of writing and spending time with his family, Ryan enjoys walking, reading and windsurfing.

Ryan is fascinated with History, Psychology and True Crime. In 2015, he finally started researching and writing his own work and at the end of the year, he released his first book on Britain's most notorious serial killer, Harold Shipman.

He has since written several books on lesser-known subjects, and taken the unique approach of writing from the killer's perspective. He narrates some of the most chilling scenes you'll encounter in the True Crime genre.

You can sign up to Ryan's newsletter to receive a free book, updates, and the latest releases at:

WWW.RYANGREENBOOKS.COM

More Books by Ryan Green

On the bloodstained floor lay an array of butcher's tools and a body without a throat, torn out by Fritz's "love bite"...

Deemed psychologically unfit to stand trial for child abuse, Fritz Haarmann was locked up in a mental asylum until a new diagnosis as "morally inferior" allowed him to walk free. His insights into the criminal underworld convinced the police to overlook his "activities" and trust him as an informant.

What harm could it do?

When the dismembered and ravaged remains of young men began to wash up on the banks of the river, a war-torn nation cowered under the threat of the man known as the Butcher, Vampire and Wolf Man.

The hunt for the killer was on, and he was hiding in plain sight.".

More Books by Ryan Green

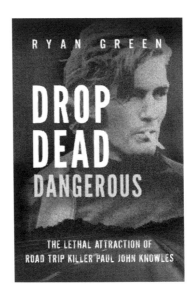

In 1974, the US East Coast was whipped up into a frenzy of fear. Locking their windows and doors, everyone was terrified of becoming the next victim of the strikingly handsome but deadly *"Casanova Killer"*. And he was on the move

After being released from jail and promptly abandoned by his fiancée, Paul John Knowles embarked on a spate of gruesome murders on a road trip up the Pacific Coast

No room for fear, no room for guilt, just the road

As the man-hunt gathered pace, the cold-blooded killing spree continued to defy detectives. With no visible pattern in the age, race nor gender of the victims, Knowle's joyride of kidnap, rape and murder tore across multiple state borders. It became a race of tragically high stakes. How many more lives would be lost before the police finally caught up.

More Books by Ryan Green

In 1861, the police of a rural French village tore their way into the woodside home of Martin Dumollard. Inside, they found chaos. Paths had been carved through mounds of bloodstained clothing, reaching as high as the ceiling in some places.

The officers assumed that the mysterious maid-robber had killed one woman but failed in his other attempts. Yet, it was becoming sickeningly clear that there was a vast gulf between the crimes they were aware of and the ones that had truly been committed.

Would Dumollard's wife expose his dark secret or was she inextricably linked to the atrocities? Whatever the circumstances, everyone was desperate to discover whether the bloody garments belonged to some of the 648 missing women.

More Books by Ryan Green

In July 1981, just days after his release from jail, Clifford Olson Junior unleashed hell on British Columbia. He kidnapped, raped, and killed six children and teenagers in a single month. While the previous missing children had been treated like runaways, there was now no question that somebody was abducting children in the Lower Mainland area, and the media went berserk.

From the age of 17, Clifford Olson Junior spent only 1,501 days outside of prison or jail. If his claims are to be believed, he averaged about one murder every 10 days. During his imprisonment, he was assessed on the Hare Psychopathy Checklist, a tool designed to evaluate psychopathy. The standard threshold is 25 to 30. He scored a 38 out of 40, the highest rating ever recorded.

More Books by Ryan Green

In 1944, as the Nazis occupied Paris, the French Police and Fire Brigade were called to investigate a vile-smelling smoke pouring out from a Parisian home. Inside, they were confronted with a scene from a nightmare. They found a factory line of bodies and multiple furnaces stocked with human remains. This was more than mere murder .

The homeowner was Dr. Marcel Petiot, an admired and charismatic physician. When questioned, Dr. Petiot claimed that he was a part of the Resistance and the bodies they discovered belonged to Nazi collaborators that he killed for the cause. The French Police, resentful of Nazi occupation and confused by a rational alternative, allowed him to leave.

Was the respected Doctor a clandestine hero fighting for national liberty or a deviant using dire domestic circumstances to his advantage? One thing is for certain, the Police and the Nazis both wanted to get their hands on Dr. Marcel Petiot to find out the truth.

More Books by Ryan Green

On 20 May 1999, the South Australian Police were called to investigate a disused bank in the unassuming town of Snowtown, in connection to the disappearance of multiple missing people. The Police were not prepared for the chilling scene that awaited them.

The officers found six barrels within the abandoned bank vault, each filled with acid and the remains of eight individuals. Accompanying the bodies were numerous everyday tools that pathologists would later confirm were used for prolonged torture, murder and cannibalism.

The findings shocked Australia to its core, which deepened still when it was revealed that the torture and murders were committed by not one, but a group of killers. The four men, led by John Bunting, targeted paedophiles, homosexuals, addicts or the 'weak' in an attempt to cleanse society.

More Books by Ryan Green

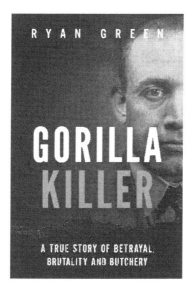

On 20th February 1926, landlady Clara Newman (60) opened her door to a potential tenant who enquired into the availability of one of her rooms. Despite his grim and bulky appearance, he introduced himself politely, in a soft-spoken voice whilst clutching a Bible in one of his large hands. She invited him in. The moment he stepped into her home, he lunged forwards, wrapping his over-sized fingers around her throat and forced her to the ground. She couldn't scream. He had learned the dangers of a scream. She slowly slipped into darkness. Given what would follow, it was probably a kindness.

The 'Gorilla Killer', Earle Nelson, roamed over 7,000 miles of North America undetected, whilst satisfying his deranged desires. During a span of almost two years, he choked the life out of more than twenty unsuspecting women, subjected their bodies to the most unspeakable acts, and seemingly enjoyed the process.

Free True Crime Audiobook

Sign up to Audible and use your free credit to download this collection of twelve books. If you cancel within 30 days, there's no charge!

WWW.RYANGREENBOOKS.COM/FREE-AUDIOBOOK

"Ryan Green has produced another excellent book and belongs at the top with true crime writers such as M. William Phelps, Gregg Olsen and Ann Rule" –**B.S. Reid**

"Wow! Chilling, shocking and totally riveting! I'm not going to sleep well after listening to this but the narration was fantastic. Crazy story but highly recommend for any true crime lover!" –**Mandy**

"Torture Mom by Ryan Green left me pretty speechless. The fact that it's a true story is just...wow" –**JStep**

"Graphic, upsetting, but superbly read and written" –**Ray C**

WWW.RYANGREENBOOKS.COM/FREE-AUDIOBOOK

Printed in Great Britain
by Amazon